Inside
the Welfare
Lobby

"Philip Mendes has written an important book about an important organisation. The debate about fairness in Australia has been hijacked by the Coalition and their army of supporters in the right-wing think tanks and sections of the media. ACOSS helps to reframe that debate. In our common quest to make Australia a fairer and more prosperous country, Mendes's book reminds us of the importance of a strong voice for the most vulnerable." *Wayne Swan, Australian Labor Party member for Lilley, and ALP Shadow Treasurer*

"This book helps to fill an acute shortage in academic writing about the major interest groups that play such a large role in Australian policy-making and politics. ACOSS stands alongside the BCA, the ACTU, the NFF and other large peak organisations; without an understanding of ACOSS our knowledge of contemporary politics is incomplete. In particular, ACOSS' role in welfare politics is central. Mendes has the best credentials of anyone I know to write such a book. His knowledge of ACOSS is up to date and detailed. This book will be a major resource for all university courses in contemporary Australian politics and a necessary guide for all informed political commentators." *John Warhurst, Professor of Politics, School of Social Sciences, Australian National University*

"Philip Mendes offers us a study of how ACOSS has built and developed its messages along with its tactics in seeking to influence policy to tackle poverty. Politicians, organisations, and researchers will all find something of interest in this examination of the case of the ACOSS and its relation to the policy making process. By studying the organisation, tensions in its role and its ability to adapt to its circumstances, alongside evaluating its successes, both around agenda setting and specific policy change to improve the position of those most disadvantaged in society, Mendes gives us not only a view into the 'black box' of policy change but an example of the strengths and weaknesses of campaigning organisations and of how their success can be judged." *Dr. Paul Dornan, Child Poverty Action Group*

Inside the Welfare Lobby

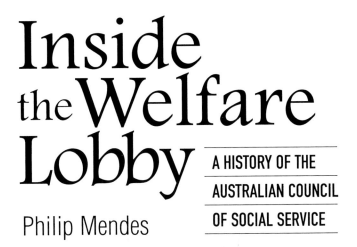

A HISTORY OF THE
AUSTRALIAN COUNCIL
OF SOCIAL SERVICE

Philip Mendes

The Role of Interest Groups in Australian Social Policy

sussex
ACADEMIC
PRESS

BRIGHTON • PORTLAND

2 4 6 8 10 9 7 5 3 1

First published 2006 in Great Britain by
SUSSEX ACADEMIC PRESS
PO Box 139
Eastbourne BN24 9BP

and in the United States of America by
SUSSEX ACADEMIC PRESS
920 NE 58th Ave   Suite 300
Portland, Oregon 97213-3786

British Library Cataloguing in Publication Data
A CIP catalogue record for this book is available from the British Library.

Library of Congress Cataloging-in-Publication Data
Mendes, Philip, 1964–
   Inside the welfare lobby : a history of the Australian
   Council of Social Service : the role of interest groups in
   Australian social policy / by Philip Mendes.
   p. cm.
   Includes bibliographical references and index.
   ISBN 1-84519-119-6 (p/b : alk. paper)
   1. Australian Council of Social Service. 2. Welfare
rights movement—Australia. 3. Pressure groups—
Australia. 4. Public welfare—Australia. 5. Welfare
state—Australia. 6. Australia—Social policy. I. Title.

HV473.M45 2006
361.80994—dc22

                                                2006014013

Typeset & Designed by SAP, Brighton & Eastbourne
Printed by The Alden Press, Malaysia
This book is printed on acid-free paper.

Contents

Acknowledgments   vi

Introduction   1

1   From Voluntary Welfare Coordination to Social Action: The early
    years of the Australian Council of Social Service, 1955–1970   7

2   Towards Social Policy Advocacy, 1970–1975   20

3   Watchdog for the Poor, 1976–1985   31

4   A Political Insider, 1985–1996   45

5   Protecting the Welfare Safety Net, 1996–2006   58

6   Labourists and Welfarists: The Relationship between the Federal
    Labor Party and the Australian Council of Social Service   72

7   Neo-Liberalism versus Social Justice: The Relationship between
    the Federal Liberal Party and the Australian Council of
    Social Service   83

8   A Natural Alliance? The Relationship between the Australian Trade
    Union movement and the Australian Council of Social Service   93

Conclusion   103

Appendix I: ACOSS leaders   105
Appendix II: ACOSS Publications   106
Appendix III: Author interviews and correspondence   115
Notes   118
Index   142

Acknowledgments

This book began its life as a Doctor of Philosophy thesis completed in the Department of Social Work at La Trobe University in 1996. I am particularly grateful to my supervisor Bob Doyle who provided enthusiastic and expert assistance with my thesis, and has remained an ongoing friend and mentor. And special thanks to the various staff and office-holders of ACOSS who have provided generous and ongoing assistance with this project whilst not always agreeing with my interpretations.

Thanks also to the people in my various policy, campaign and academic networks who have encouraged me to continue blending scholarship with activism. They include most notably Susie Bunn, Linda Briskman, Lea Campbell, Gavin Dufty, Catherine Forbes, Mark Furlong, Chris Goddard, Melanie Landau, Tony Levy, Delia O'Donohue, Don Siemon, Paul Smyth, and Mark Zirnsak. Thanks also to the numerous Monash University social work staff and students who have alternatively challenged, frustrated and inspired over the past eight years.

I am also grateful to my publisher Anthony Grahame of Sussex Academic Press for his friendly and enthusiastic co-operation and assistance, and to John Warhurst, Paul Dornan and Wayne Swan for their generous pre-publication endorsements of this text. Many thanks also to Ian McAllister from the *Australian Journal of Political Science* and Frank Stilwell from the *Journal of Australian Political Economy* respectively for kindly allowing me to include as chapter 6 (AJPS) and chapters 7 and 8 (JAPE) revised versions of three earlier articles that appeared in their journals.

Above all, I would like to thank my cherished wife Tamar Lewit who has provided, as always, the constant and unqualified encouragement, support and stimulation needed to complete the project; my darling daughter Miranda and son Lucas for constantly reminding me that life is a wonderful and exciting journey; and my dear mother for her life long support of my scholarly endeavours.

Introduction

This book explores the history and activities of the peak lobby group of the community welfare sector, the Australian Council of Social Service (ACOSS). ACOSS has played a central role in the welfare politics debate as the foremost defender of the Australian welfare state, and is widely recognized as one of the more important lobby groups in this country. Yet whilst some previous writers have briefly looked at welfare politics and the activities of ACOSS, this is the first study to comprehensively examine the role played by ACOSS in the Australian social policy debate.

ACOSS was originally formed as a peak coordinating body of welfare service providers similar to that of overseas peak bodies such as the British National Council of Voluntary Organizations. However, over time, ACOSS shifted its emphasis from representing the specific interests of its member organizations to advocating for the broad interests of low income and disadvantaged Australians.[1] Consequently, ACOSS devotes most of its resources to promoting the elimination of poverty and the establishment of a fairer and more equitable society which will enhance the life opportunities and living standards of low income earners. It also supports the role of community welfare organizations both in terms of their provision of services to disadvantaged Australians, and their contribution to national policy debates.

Structurally, ACOSS is made up of almost seventy membership organizations including the eight Councils of Social Service in each of the States and Territories; national peak organisations of both consumers and service providers; national religious and secular welfare agencies such as the Salvation Army, Mission Australia and the Smith Family; key professional associations such as those of social workers and psychologists and peak bodies which specialize in particular policy areas or population groups such as National Shelter; and low-income consumer groups such as the Carers Association of Australia, People with Disability Australia, Australian Pensioners and Superannuants Federation and the National Council for the Single Mother and her Child. ACOSS also has over four hundred associate members consisting of individuals and state or locally-based organizations.

The organizations represented in ACOSS' membership are significant groupings whether measured in narrow monetary or broader societal terms. It was estimated in 1999–2000 that community welfare organizations had an annual expenditure of $7000 million, and employed more than 215,000 people.[2] At the same time it is important to acknowledge that ACOSS and the community welfare sector are not necessarily synonymous either in terms of their resources or their philosophical objectives.

ACOSS is based in Sydney, but all states are represented on the honorary ACOSS Board of Governors. The Board consists of 20 members including a President and a Treasurer who are directly elected every two years by the whole membership; 16 other elected persons of whom six are elected by the National Member Organizations, two are elected by the Special Assembly which comprises consumer groups who are member organizations, and eight nominated by the State and Territory Councils of Social Service; and two members co-opted by the Board.

ACOSS is currently active in ten overlapping policy portfolio areas: community services; economics and tax; employment, education and training; health; housing; indigenous issues; international issues; law and justice; rural and remote communities; and social security. The development of policy and advocacy in all these areas is coordinated by an honorary principal policy adviser who is backed up by a number of other policy specialists. These policy groups underpin ACOSS' development of critical policy analysis and strategies.

ACOSS is largely an organization of middle-class welfare professionals which acts on behalf of low income people. Most of its key leaders have held prominent paid or voluntary roles in large community welfare organizations and/or been active in the State and Territory Councils of Social Service. ACOSS' claim as a professional advocacy body to represent the interests of low income and disadvantaged Australians has frequently been questioned by governments, and sometimes by the poor themselves.[3] One reason for this is that ACOSS has often struggled to satisfactorily involve consumer groups in its policy development and decision-making. This has been particularly the case with the unemployed, although that is not to deny the structural difficulties involved in ensuring such representation. Such groups often feel stigmatized by their status, and tend to move in and out of the workforce. Nevertheless, ACOSS today has managed to ensure formal representation for the major existing low income consumer groups within its organizational structure.

The inter-organizational dynamics of ACOSS have also changed over time. As discussed in chapters 1 to 5, ACOSS has experienced numerous internal disputes reflecting a range of ideological and personal rivalries.

However, ACOSS seem in the last two decades to have established a consensus around key issues such as the division of labour between paid staff and elected officers, and the choice of public spokespersons. Today ACOSS presents a unified voice to the outside world which arguably contributes to its external legitimacy.

Ideologically, ACOSS can be broadly described as a social justice organization which emphasizes tackling the structural causes of poverty and inequality. Both secular social democratic ideology and Christian social teachings have exerted a significant influence on ACOSS' political position in favour of a broad redistribution of income from the rich to the poor. To be sure, ACOSS has a highly diverse membership ranging philosophically from consumer groups representing single mothers and people living with HIV/AIDS to traditional Christian charities which may hold relatively conservative agendas on social issues such as sexuality, abortion and illicit drugs. Nevertheless, ACOSS remains united in its support for a publicly funded welfare safety net complemented by a progressive taxation system.

As noted in chapters 2 to 5, ACOSS has experienced ideological attacks from both the political Left and Right. Some on the Left have criticized ACOSS for allegedly keeping its arguments within the framework of the dominant economic rationalist discourse. Traditional Marxists go further, arguing that ACOSS' support for the welfare state has misled and disarmed the working class, especially low income earners and social security beneficiaries. Such authors call on ACOSS to overthrow the capitalist welfare state, rather than attempting to wield it as a weapon on behalf of the poor.[4]

These criticisms arguably have some legitimacy in that ACOSS has often narrowed its critique to the government's specific priorities, rather than rejecting the overall economic rationalist model, and presenting an alternative structural agenda. Nevertheless, it is also likely that stronger criticism of the government's overall agenda would lead to ACOSS' complete isolation from the political mainstream.

It would appear that this leftist critique of ACOSS (which has all but disappeared from public discourse in the last decade) is explicitly linked to the broader debate around representation for the poor. In short, the question to be answered is whether the interests of low income earners are best represented by mainstream government-funded lobby groups such as ACOSS linked to the traditional welfare state, or alternatively by radical activist/protest groups utilizing more confrontational methods and strategies and committed both to financial and political independence from government agendas?[5] It is arguable that an effective anti-poverty movement requires both these forms of advocacy.[6]

More politically influential in recent decades has been the neo-liberal critique of the welfare lobby based on public choice theory. This critique holds that advocacy groups such as ACOSS represent self-interested professionals concerned with building well-paid careers rather than with genuinely assisting the poor.[7] However, this critique seems to be misinformed given that ACOSS' lobbying activities focus on promoting higher incomes and opportunities for welfare consumers, rather than grabbing more resources for welfare organizations and programs.

Overall, the public choice critique of ACOSS appears more concerned with specifically delegitimizing the agendas of those groups that seek increased government spending, than with genuinely reducing the privileges of self-interested lobby groups.[8]

ACOSS describes itself as a non-party political organization committed to dialogue with all political parties. This means that they do not seek a formal alliance with any particular government or political party which may lead to a diminution of their own political choices. Rather, they aim to influence all parties to develop policies which benefit people affected by poverty and inequality. On balance, ACOSS appear to have traditionally enjoyed closer relations with the Labor Party, rather than with the Liberal/National Coalition, due to the greater symmetry of their ideological positions. But as we note in chapters 6 and 7, relationships with governments of both political sides have always involved a mixture of co-operation and criticism.

ACOSS is both proactive and reactive. ACOSS is proactive in that it independently develops and promotes policy ideas based on the experiences, priorities and concerns of its constituency and membership as a means of raising public awareness and influencing policy change. And ACOSS is reactive in terms of responding to proposals by government, political parties, the media, and other key players in the policy making process.[9]

In its relations with government, ACOSS operates as an "insider" lobbying group concerned to retain an ongoing consultative status. This means they typically engage in certain types of accepted lobbying activities.[10] ACOSS is not able to employ the economic sanctions (e.g. strike action or disinvestment) open to producer groups such as business and unions.[11] This means that ACOSS are likely to be successful only when their agenda does not clash fundamentally with that of the government.

ACOSS also have a limited capacity to mobilize their own membership behind specific policy positions given the voluntaristic nature of their membership structure.[12] For example, ACOSS could in principle recommend that its membership initiate a confrontational strategy such as a welfare industry strike in a sensitive area such as the Job Network. However, in practice, it is unlikely that ACOSS would attempt to do so given that ACOSS members would be under no obligation to follow such a directive.

Consequently, ACOSS primarily use co-operation and persuasion strategies, rather than contest strategies, to promote change. ACOSS generally adhere to a number of key strategies identified as crucial for lobbying success. These include the provision of well-researched case studies, professional expertise, speaking with a united and representative voice, topicality and timing in its interventions, moderate and considered recommendations, and an emphasis on broader national concerns rather than narrow self-interest.[13]

ACOSS uses a range of lobbying activities including submissions to and meetings with leading public servants and government ministers, presentations to parliamentary inquiries and hearings, meetings with internal party policy committees, addresses to public forums, and occasionally public pressure campaigns. ACOSS also maintain extensive contact with the media since media coverage can be crucial in influencing government policy outcomes, and engage in alliances with other important lobby groups such as trade unions (see discussion in chapter 8), the churches, environmental groups, and sometimes the business sector. ACOSS also aim to influence general public opinion.

Political influence and effectiveness are often difficult concepts to measure. Effectiveness is generally defined as the ability of lobby groups to cite specific policy reforms or changes emanating from their advocacy.[14] However, in this study, we will extend the term to refer to more subtle achievements such as placing issues on the public policy agenda and maintaining their visibility.

Using this definition, we would judge ACOSS to have been an effective lobby group over time, particularly given the dominant neo-liberal agenda of the last 20 years. As we note in chapters 1 to 5, ACOSS appears to have been successful in defending the fundamental structures of the welfare state from attack, and in protecting its low income constituency from potentially greater hardship and distress. However, it has arguably had only minimal success in convincing governments to introduce measures that would lead to greater social or economic equity.[15]

ACOSS relies on an annual government grant for about 45 per cent of its funding. Other major contributions to ACOSS' current income of just over one million dollars come from membership fees and donations (about 25 per cent), annual congress income (about 10 per cent), project management and fees for services (about 10 per cent), and publications income (about 7 per cent).

The advantage of continued government funding is that it facilitates relative financial certainty. However, financial reliance on government may potentially compromise ACOSS' independence, and prevent it from speaking out against government policies.[16] In addition, ACOSS' relatively minimal resources limit its lobbying capacity compared to other better funded lobby groups representing business and trade unions. ACOSS has long recognized the danger of its limited funding base, and is progressively seeking to diversify and expand its sources of income.

ACOSS has proven to be both a dynamic and resilient body over the 50 years of its existence. It has had to reinvent itself on a number of occasions in order to successfully confront and overcome various political, ideological, representational, organizational, and resource challenges. It will no doubt face many new challenges in the future, and we discuss some of them in the concluding chapter.

1

From Voluntary Welfare Coordination to Social Action

The early years of the Australian Council of Social Service, 1955–1970

The Australian Council of Social Service (ACOSS) is today one of the best known lobby groups in the country. Yet ACOSS' beginnings were far more humble. The Council was formed as a coordinating body for the voluntary welfare sector modeled on the UK National Council of Social Services (now called the National Council of Voluntary Organizations),[1] and aimed to become a major contributor to enhanced welfare policies and programs. However, for the first decade of its existence, ACOSS enjoyed no financial support from government, lived in a borrowed office, pursued little social action, and survived only due to the generosity of its affiliates and supporters.

The first annual grant from the Commonwealth Government in 1966 facilitated the transformation of ACOSS into a more influential and activist-oriented organization. This was reflected in the campaign for more effective health insurance policies, and in ongoing advocacy around income security benefits. By 1970, ACOSS had shifted towards the Canadian Council for Social Development model which emphasized broader social policy goals beyond the specific interests of the voluntary sector including advocacy on behalf of welfare consumers.[2]

The Beginnings of the Councils of Social Service Movement

The Australian welfare state has always been based on a mixed economy of service provision. This economy includes four sets of institutions: employers who are responsible for wage rates and conditions of employment; the market or private sector which is involved in the commercial provision of services such as health, education and housing; voluntary agencies; and the informal sector where care is provided by families and individuals.[3]

Voluntary agencies including church groups and other private charities have historically played a central role in the provision of health services and other social programs. These agencies were always subsidized by government, but were able to provide services cheaply due to the assistance of thousands of volunteers. However, the advent of the Depression and World War Two, and the rapid growth of the Commonwealth government welfare sector (particularly during the period of the Chifley Australian Labor Party government), produced some significant changes in the voluntary sector.

One important change was the movement away from traditional moral judgments of the poor towards newer social and psychological theories. Another key change was the gradual replacement of traditional volunteer charity workers with a professional workforce headed by trained social workers.[4] These changes drove the establishment of Councils of Social Service in most Australian states in the nineteen forties and fifties. Their creation also reflected the concern of the leading voluntary agencies to maintain their influence on government welfare policy and planning. Equally, most state governments remained dependent on non-government agencies to fulfil the bulk of their statutory welfare responsibilities, and hence welcomed greater coordination within the sector.[5]

The founders of the State Councils included a diverse range of personalities and viewpoints. On the one hand, many of the leading office holders appear to have been members of the "charity elite", establishment figures with an interest in charity matters.[6] In Adelaide, for example, a combination of knights, ladies, reverends and doctors participated in the South Australian Council of Social Service together with the Lord Mayor of Adelaide, the Minister and Director of Education, the Commissioner of Police, and other local notables.[7] Similarly, representatives of the Psychiatrists' Association, the judiciary, and "other learned professions" were prominent in the establishment of the Queensland Council of Social

Service,[8] whilst Lady Herring, wife of the Lieutenant-Governor, became the first President of the Victorian Council.[9]

On the other hand, the fledgling social work profession – represented organizationally by the Australian Association of Social Workers (AASW) – played a key role in both the creation and ongoing activities of the Councils.[10] Social workers generally rejected moralistic charitable concepts such as "genuine need" and "the undeserving" poor, and instead influenced the Councils towards a holistic understanding of the social and structural aspects of poverty.[11]

For example, the NSW Council of Social Service aimed to "study social conditions, problems and community facilities", and to "stimulate community action and influence social legislation".[12] Similarly, the Victorian Council targeted broad social concerns such as homelessness, the plight of Aborigines, the assimilation of immigrants, alcoholism, and the training of child care workers.[13]

Moves Towards A National Welfare Council

In the late nineteen forties and early fifties, moves were made by the fast expanding Commonwealth Department of Social Services to initiate the formation of a National Social Welfare Committee which would act as an adviser to the Minister of Social Services, and seek affiliation with the International Conference of Social Work (later known as the International Council on Social Welfare). The Department was concerned to prevent overlapping of services, promote enhanced training of social welfare professionals, and facilitate greater cooperation between the voluntary and statutory sectors.[14]

These moves received support from a number of sources including the Australian Association of Social Workers, the Australian Red Cross Society, and the University Departments of Social Studies. The AASW, in particular, was keen to heighten its profile within the international social work community. However, little progress was made due to opposition from State Governments, and differences of opinion regarding the type of organization to be formed.[15]

An Australian Council of Social Service was formed in 1951 in order to coordinate the activities of the State Councils of Social Service, and create Councils in States or Territories where they did not exist. The Australian Council was also intended to act as a "liaison with comparable bodies overseas".[16] However, this Council failed to meet its objective of acting as a recognized national welfare committee. Nor did the Council succeed in acquiring affiliation with the International Conference of Social Work. After the creation of the Australian Social Welfare Council (later to be renamed ACOSS), the Australian Council of Social Service was voluntarily disbanded in 1958.

Following these initial failures, two meetings were held in Melbourne in June and August 1955 under the auspices of the Department of Social Services to discuss plans for the formation of a Council national in character and covering significant phases of social work in Australia carried out by governments and voluntary bodies. The Minister for Social Services, William McMahon, stated his support for the proposed Council, and also indicated that the government would provide some financial support.[17]

However, on the day of the second meeting, the Director General of the Department Frank Rowe (who was organized to chair proceedings) withdrew unexpectedly under instructions from the Social Services Minister. This incident was to prove symbolic of the ongoing difficulties that ACOSS would face in securing any recognition or support from the Commonwealth Government. Nevertheless, those present decided to proceed with the formation of the Council, and the Reverend Darcy O'Reilly, representing the Methodist Church of Australia, was elected the inaugural President.[18]

Following this inauspicious beginning, a provisional committee for the Australian Social Welfare Council was set up, and the Council was formally established in April 1956. Its first home was the use of a room in the Social Work Department of the University of Sydney which it had to vacate when lectures were conducted. A mailing address was provided by the Australian Services Canteen Trust, the organization concerned with the welfare of ex-serviceman.[19] In 1959, the Council changed its name to the Australian Council of Social Service.

The Membership and Objectives of ACOSS

Twenty-three organizations affiliated as inaugural members of the Australian Social Welfare Council. They included the national bodies of the three principal religious denominations, Protestant, Catholic and Jewish, the Salvation Army, the national bodies of the war widows and civilian widows, the YMCA and YWCA, representatives of women and nurses, the British (later Australian) Medical Association, the Australian Association of Social Workers, the Schools of Social Work, and the four existing State Councils of Social Service.[20] Other subsequently acquired members included the Red Cross, the Methodist Church, the Australian Psychological

Society, Professor Ronald Henderson's Institute of Applied Economic Research, and the Association of Apex Clubs.

These organizations represented a diverse range of views and interests. However, there were arguably three key sources of power and influence within ACOSS: 1) The large religious welfare agencies and conservative charities; 2) The doctors; and 3) The professional social workers. These three groups also contributed disproportionately to the financing of the Council.[21]

Accordingly, the four Presidents of ACOSS during this period – Reverend Darcy O'Reilly (1956–57), Professor Morven Brown (1957–1961), Dr John Hunter (1961–1964), and Major General Roy Gordon (1964–1970) – represented respectively the Methodist Church, the Schools of Social Work, the Australian Medical Association, and the Services Canteens Trust Fund (SCTF). The SCTF, which represented large numbers of ex-servicemen and their wives and dependants, was particularly influential.[22] In addition, the major committee positions also tended to be held by representatives of these three groups. For example, social workers Norma Parker and Helen James (representing a number of different organizations) both played prominent long-term roles in the local and international activities of ACOSS. The State Councils of Social Service were also significant, but often in a negative way given their competing agendas, and their reluctance to share their sources of influence and funding with the national body.[23]

The breadth of membership meant that ACOSS adopted a broad community welfare orientation that went beyond narrow charitable concerns. To be sure, there was some particular concern with representing the interests of the voluntary welfare sector *vis-à-vis* both State and Commonwealth governments. For example, the inaugural ASWC Annual Report emphasized that voluntary welfare services remained significant in spite of the expansion of Commonwealth government programs. But the ASWC also called for greater integration of voluntary and statutory welfare services, better social welfare planning, and improved services for widows, Aborigines, the mentally ill, and deprived children.[24]

The amended 1959 Constitution reflected this community welfare agenda. ACOSS sought to promote assistance to the needy, to improve services designed to relieve poverty, distress, sickness or helplessness, to carry out research to alleviate poverty and distress, and to promote the establishment of new services in the areas of health, migrant support, and juvenile delinquency.[25] A later statement referred similarly to promoting a critical evaluation of existing welfare services, and to stimulating the establishment of new services where required.[26]

And in 1966, the ACOSS Executive Officer, Hope Clayton, emphasized the importance of moving beyond charitable assistance to the needy to "attacking the causes of need". According to Clayton, ACOSS should be involved in "the continued study of social change, of the current relevance of social welfare policies, of legislation by which these are implemented, and of the attitude of the community to different social problems".[27]

But equally, it could be argued that ACOSS failed for most of this period to move beyond representing the interests of the voluntary welfare sector, or to advocate anything other than residual welfare programs focused solely on the poor and disadvantaged. There was little discussion of universalistic approaches that defined welfare as a right for all, regardless of income or position. And noticeably with the exception of the civilian widows and war widows, there were no consumer affiliates within ACOSS representing low-income people. This was despite the concern expressed as early as the 1960 National Conference that ACOSS aim to represent the political interests of the poor and disadvantaged.[28]

However, in the late 1960s and early 1970s, ACOSS broadened its membership to include newer activist and consumer groups including the Australian Union of Students, Community Aid Abroad, the Australian Council for the Single Mother and Her Child, and ABSCHOL (Aboriginal Scholarship Scheme). In addition, social activists such as David Scott from the Brotherhood of St Laurence, Marie Coleman and Murray Geddes from the Australian Association of Social Workers, and multicultural advocate Walter Lippmann became prominent in the Association.[29]

These changes in membership both coincided with and influenced ACOSS' shift from the older UK Council of National Service model to a newer model based on the Canadian Council of Social Development's concern with broader social policy goals. The Canadian model was reflected in ACOSS' adoption of a universalistic welfare state model based on improving general social and living standards in the broad areas of income, employment, education, health, housing and recreation, whilst maintaining a particular concern with the living standards of vulnerable groups.[30] ACOSS had moved away from representing principally the needs of the voluntary welfare sector towards becoming an advocacy group for low income earners.

ACOSS' relationship with the Commonwealth Government

For much of this period, ACOSS defined itself as a coordinating body seeking to act in partnership with government, rather than as a lobby group aiming to represent the interests of the voluntary welfare sector with government. For example in 1960, the ACOSS Chairman Professor Morven Brown emphasized ACOSS' commitment to consultation with government: "This Council feels that it could usefully reflect social work opinion to the government and equally interpret government opinion to the public".[31]

Yet although the primary initiative for the establishment of ACOSS had come from the Commonwealth Department of Social Services, the government seems to have regarded the Council with a lack of interest or even disfavor for the first decade of its existence. This attitude seems to have reflected a number of factors including a reluctance on the part of the Commonwealth to consult with the non-government sector on policy and program development, and also a perception that ACOSS would potentially use any formal government recognition to act as a lobby group for increased government spending on welfare services.[32] This government disinterest contrasted with the active involvement of state welfare departments in the respective state Councils of Social Service. Perhaps the key factor here was that state governments were used to collaborating with the voluntary welfare sector in providing welfare services, whereas few similar collaborative arrangements existed at the national level.

The lack of support from government had significant negative ramifications for ACOSS. Firstly, government statutory welfare organizations were prevented from affiliating with ACOSS on the grounds that their presence would prejudice the independent character of the Council in that public servants were not free agents and would be able to speak only as government policy dictated. The Director-General of the Department of Social Services Frank Rowe declined an offer to act as patron of ACOSS, arguing that if "ACOSS wanted to bring pressure on the Government, it would be awkward if there were government representatives in their midst"[33] As a result, the ACOSS constitution made no provision for participation by the Commonwealth Government. But the absence of Commonwealth statutory agencies arguably limited the legitimacy of ACOSS' claim to speak on behalf of the welfare sector.[34]

And even more importantly, the government refused to provide any financial support to ACOSS except for meeting the Council's affiliation fee with the International Conference of Social Work (ICSW). This meant that no funding was available for interstate travel for delegates, or for the Executive Officer. In addition, no funding was provided for ACOSS representatives to attend international meetings held by the ICSW even though the desire for active Australian participation in the ICSW had been a major factor behind ACOSS' formation.

ACOSS was left with a shoestring budget which prevented the Council from operating as an effective national coordinating body. For example, ACOSS' annual income in 1964–65 was only 1,572 pounds. In contrast, both the NSW and Victorian Councils of Social Service enjoyed major state government subsidies, and had incomes of approximately 5,000 pounds.[35]

According to Major-General Roy Gordon, who was Treasurer of ACOSS from 1957–1964, "ACOSS could not afford an office or staff or even pay fares for attendance at meetings. We barely had enough money for stamps and stationery. The Council decided to charge a subscription for member-ship, but this had to be not so large that organizations would not join or cause them to leave. We could not go out to raise funds as the only source of fund raising was in the states, and the State Councils of Social Service would not agree to us going into their fields to raise money. As a result, prac-tically all the work for the Council was done by the Honorary Secretary, Miss Jean Anderson and myself. After a considerable time, we were able to afford a part-time Secretary on a very low fee – first Eileen Davidson, and later Hope Clayton. All the office work including postage over these years was put through the Services Canteen Trust Fund office with the approval of the Trustees. It was entirely due to the SCTF that the Council functioned at all".[36]

Nevertheless, occasional discussions were held with the government and relevant Ministers. However, these discussions focused primarily on broader policy issues such as the rate of aged pensions, retrenchment of social workers in the Commonwealth Department of Immigration, and marriage guidance legislation. There was little progress towards meeting ACOSS' concern that it be formally recognized as a consultative body engaged in providing advice to government. For example in 1961, Prime Minister Menzies refused to meet an ACOSS delegation, and stated that ACOSS was not considered a suitable body for a government subsidy.[37]

Finally in 1966, ACOSS presented a submission for financial support to the Prime Minister. ACOSS was subsequently awarded a grant of $15,000 per year for three years consisting of $5,000 for international activities, and $10,000 on a matching basis provided ACOSS raised an equivalent amount from its own sources.[38] This grant enabled ACOSS to set up a Secretariat with a full time Secretary and a small staff. The grant was accompanied by increasing government interest in the work of ACOSS including the atten-dance of a government observer at ACOSS Board meetings.

Successive Ministers for Social Services, Ian Sinclair and William Wentworth, the Director General of Social Services Mr Hamilton, the Minister for Health Dr A. J. Forbes, and the Minister for Immigration Bill Snedden all established cooperative relationships with ACOSS. For example, Sinclair addressed the 1966 ACOSS National Conference, and Wentworth addressed both the 1968 and 1970 National Conferences. In addition, a representative of the Department of Social Services – Max Wryell – was appointed to attend Council meetings on an observer basis.[39]

According to Ian Sinclair, ACOSS was one of several community welfare organizations recognized by government, but "was not as significant as some other groups such as the Australian Council for the Ageing, the Civilian Widows and War Widows, the Pensioners' Association, the RSL, and the ACTU. Yet it enjoyed access to me and the department equal to other community groups. Representatives met with me to discuss social welfare issues on a number of occasions".[40] William Wentworth recalls "frequent informal contacts with ACOSS". He regarded ACOSS as an "excellent" body, and regretted that Treasury policy "impeded better cooperation between ACOSS and the government".[41]

Major ACOSS Activities

Despite limited resources, ACOSS was still able to participate in a number of important local and international activities. For example, large ACOSS delegations regularly attended the biennial conferences of the International Conference of Social Work, and a number of ACOSS representatives including Reverend Darcy O'Reilly, Dr John Hunter, and Professor John Lawrence were appointed to important roles within the ICSW. In addition, ACOSS collaborated with the National Welfare Committees of the United Kingdom, USA and Canada in undertaking a study of eight English social welfare terms, provided a training course on child welfare programs for visiting social welfare personnel from Asian and African countries, and provided social work supervision for overseas social work students.

Other activities pertained to the coordination and enhancement of the local voluntary welfare sector. For example, ACOSS contributed along with interested national youth organizations to the formation of a National Youth Council. ACOSS also played a role in the creation of Citizens' Advice Bureau in Australia, undertook a pilot study of the resources available to voluntary welfare agencies in Victoria, protested the retrenchment of social workers from the Commonwealth Department of Immigration, attempted to promote tax concessions for non-government welfare agencies, and established a Joint Committee with the AASW to promote more effective training programs for social welfare personnel.

ACOSS began publication in 1964 of a quarterly newsletter titled ACOSS Quarterly, and later assumed responsibility for publication of the Australian Journal of Social Issues. In addition, ACOSS organized major biannual national welfare conferences from 1960 onwards. These conferences focused on such issues as Social Welfare in Australia (1960), Urban and Rural Community Development (1962), The National Income and Social

Welfare (1964), The Voluntary Principle in Community Welfare (1966), Welfare of Ethnic Minorities (1968), and Social Welfare in the 1970s (1970).

Other ACOSS activities pertained to broader debates and agendas. For example, ACOSS concerns included improved accommodation for the disabled, greater employment opportunities for the physically handicapped, equality for Aborigines, promotion of quality service delivery in areas such as adoption and marriage guidance, improved standards for day care centers for children of working mothers, improvements to hire purchase legislation, higher age pensions, financial assistance for deserted wives and wives of prisoners, and improved payments for married men on sickness benefit or unemployment benefit. By 1970, ACOSS was arguing for a national review of social welfare provisions.[42]

ACOSS were also represented on the Commonwealth Immigration Advisory Council, and formed a Joint Migration Committee with the Australian Council for Overseas Aid to promote improved support services for migrants including mental health services. Headed by Walter Lippmann, this Committee was an early and influential source of support for the ideas of multiculturalism.[43]

Towards a Social Action Agenda

From the beginning, ACOSS planned to undertake research and social action projects that would influence welfare policies and agendas. For example, the first ACOSS annual report canvassed potential projects pertaining to widows, Aborigines, the mentally ill, and socially deprived children.[44] A later annual report emphasized the necessity for social research that would address social inequalities.[45] In addition, a number of featured speakers at the 1960 ACOSS National Conference urged ACOSS to participate in social action to attack the structural causes of poverty.[46] However, this ambition was severely curtailed by the limited resources available.

ACOSS' first major research study, *Widows in Australia* (see further details below), was conducted under the auspices of the NSW Council of Social Service with significant financial assistance from the Services Canteens Trust Fund. Nevertheless, the Widows study was an exception to the rule. It wasn't until the receipt of the 1966 government grant that ACOSS developed the capacity to undertake regular social action campaigns.

ACOSS was also influenced by the rediscovery of poverty in the mid-late 1960s by Professor Ronald Henderson and other academic and community researchers.[47] In addition, ACOSS began to attract new affiliates and activists (particularly via the Victorian Council of Social Service) who were committed to public advocacy on poverty and related issues. ACOSS started to shift away from merely representing the concerns of the non-government sector to also address the interests of welfare consumers.

For example, ACOSS launched a joint campaign with the Australian Association of Social Workers in 1968 for more effective health insurance provisions. Utilizing research undertaken by hospital social workers, they issued a joint statement calling for a full-scale inquiry into the problems of the chronically ill, an increasing proportion of whom were in the younger age group. ACOSS argued that the existing hospital and medical benefits scheme failed to meet the needs of the most vulnerable groups – the chronically ill and families on low incomes. ACOSS urged that consideration be given to introducing a government-controlled compulsory health insurance scheme that would be available to all, with contributions varying according to income.[48]

The joint ACOSS/AASW report received enormous media coverage, and appears to have played an important role in the reforms introduced by the Gorton Government in 1969 on hospital and medical insurance for patients with chronic conditions.[49]

ACOSS also began to issue annual pre-Budget submissions on social service benefits. For example, they argued for increases in the rates of unemployment and sickness benefits in order to prevent families from living in poverty. However, these submissions appeared to have little influence on government policy.

A former Department of Social Services Director-General Max Wryell would later comment: "ACOSS' policy pronouncements and Budget statements in its early years were pretty waffly. In many cases, they were made after the Budget had been brought down or at least after decisions had been made but not yet been announced. The ACOSS comments also seemed to be made in the assumption that the sky was the limit as far as funds for social welfare were concerned. There was no suggestion for priorities of need hence it was easy for governments and bureaucracies to dismiss the ACOSS proposals".[50]

Some of these social action campaigns provoked considerable tension and division within ACOSS. For example, the Australian Medical Association was offended by ACOSS' endorsement of a compulsory health insurance scheme, and other affiliates attacked this policy as allegedly aligning ACOSS with the Australian Labor Party.[51] There was also continuing concern that ACOSS seek to engage with rather than criticize the government, and that any use of the media be limited for fear of upsetting the government. For example, on one occasion, ACOSS was acutely embarrassed that a pre-Budget submission was released to and publicized in the press without the Minister's prior permission.[52] Two members of the

ACOSS Board – Roy Gordon and Lloyd Phillips – sought an immediate appointment with the Director-General of the Department of Social Security in order to "clear the air".[53]

Overall, ACOSS in 1970 remained a body committed to consensual rather than confrontational strategies, to consultation and cooperation with government, and mostly to behind-the-scenes lobbying based on "private submissions and a quiet word to those in high places",[54] rather than public and media campaigns. It was still primarily a body concerned with promoting more effective knowledge of, coordination of, and planning of, social welfare needs and programs locally and internationally,[55] rather than with undertaking lobbying activities on behalf of welfare consumers. However, this approach would fundamentally change with the appointment of the experienced child welfare researcher Joan Brown as Executive Officer/Secretary-General.

Case Study of Social Action: Widows in Australia

For some years welfare agencies had been concerned at the financial plight of civilian widows with children. The evidence suggested that many widows required emergency relief including food, clothing, help with debts and housing assistance on a regular basis. In 1959, the New South Wales Council of Social Service commenced a study of the social and economic condition of widows with dependent children at the invitation of the Australian Council of Social Service. The study examined the following aspects of widowed life: occupation and employment, housing, finances, the needs of children going to high school, the use made of social agencies, health, the effect of widowhood on social life, and problems in bringing up children alone.

The Study, which was based on a random sample of widows in the Sydney Metropolitan area and a survey of widows in two NSW country towns, found that civilian widows and deserted mothers often experienced severe poverty, particularly when compared with war widows who enjoyed much higher incomes. For example, 14 per cent of widowed mothers had no money left after paying rent and food while a further 38 per cent had less than one pound left each week after these basic expenses. Widows with three or more children, and those with children of pre-school age were particularly disadvantaged. The study recommended an increase in the basic rate of pension for widows.[56]

ACOSS established an Action Planning Committee in order to pressure the government to take action. Initially, ACOSS sent complimentary copies of the report to a selected group of 46 Commonwealth parliamentarians. The report was received favorably by both government and opposition MPs, and a number of positive references were made to it in Parliament.[57] ACOSS then sought to influence public opinion via circulating a publicity brochure titled "50,000 Children in Australia have no Father" to legislators, local government, welfare agencies, women's groups, the media, and the affiliates of State Councils of Social Service. There was some publicity on radio and television, and ACOSS also held public meetings to highlight the plight of civilian widows with dependent children.[58] The campaign persuaded the Commonwealth Government to increase the pension for civilian widows by three pounds a week through the introduction of a Mothers Allowance in the August 1963 Budget.[59]

Conclusion

Voluntary welfare agencies have always played a key role in the Australian mixed welfare economy. Whilst the growth of Commonwealth state welfare in the 1940s led to greater government control over welfare policy, the voluntary sector remained central to the provision of services and programs. Within this changing political context, ACOSS was formed as a coordinating body of voluntary welfare agencies concerned to assist government to promote more effective welfare planning and services. An associated aim was to represent the interests of the voluntary sector including the professional groups employed in that sector.

Over time, ACOSS gradually shifted its agenda, and began to address the interests of welfare consumers. By 1970, ACOSS had taken steps towards addressing broader social policy goals, and becoming an advocacy body for low-income earners.

Questions for Discussion

➤ Discuss the reasons for the formation of ACOSS.

➤ Which groups in society did ACOSS claim to represent?

➤ Why did it take so long for ACOSS to develop a social action agenda?

2

Towards Social Policy Advocacy, 1970–1975

The early to mid 1970s was a time of significant change and reform in Australian social policy. The Henderson Commission of Inquiry into Poverty and the extensive social spending of the Whitlam Labor Government influenced a core shift in ACOSS' agendas and modes of operation. ACOSS moved away from its traditional role as a relatively quiet coordinating body representing the large non-government charities, and instead became an increasingly outspoken and activist social policy body advocating for the interests of low income earners and other welfare consumers.[1]

ACOSS' increased professionalism played an important role in this transition. The appointment of Joan Brown as the first full-time Secretary-General in June 1970 facilitated a substantial expansion of ACOSS activities. Long-time ACOSS staffer Joan McClintock recalls that Brown's arrival was "quite revolutionary. Hope Clayton (former ACOSS Executive Officer) was the model of the old-type radical social worker. She got paid an absolute pittance and was penny-pinching in saving money. She did all the photocopying and typing herself, whereas Joan would refuse to do these things, but devise means of raising money to employ people to make ACOSS a more effective and professional organization".[2]

Brown devised a specific strategy to raise public and media awareness of social policy issues. This strategy involved the publication and dissemination of ACOSS social policy documents including production of a new quarterly magazine *Australian Social Welfare* from March 1971 onwards which succeeded *ACOSS Quarterly*, the location and distribution of other Australian material, and the dissemination of overseas material (mainly British and Canadian) which discussed social issues and social programmes from a variety of viewpoints.[3] In addition, ACOSS established a series of

Standing Committees on Family and Child Welfare, Health Services and Housing and Urban and Regional Development (as well as updating existing committees on Economic Factors and Social Welfare, and Migrant Welfare) which attracted a wider group of academics and community activists.[4]

According to Brown, "we can claim at least some of the credit for the awakening of the social welfare sector which was evident from 1971 onwards and for the flow on this had to the media and the general public. We were not of course the only influence".[5]

Another important factor was the changing nature of the ACOSS membership and leadership. ACOSS broadened its membership base, attracting consumer organizations representing single mothers, the disabled and pensioners. Other new affiliates included the Australian Association for the Mentally Retarded, the Smith Family, the Family Planning Association of Australia, the Child and Family Welfare Council of Australia, the Australian Multiple Sclerosis Society, the Legacy Co-ordinating Council, the Inter Church Trade and Industry Mission, the Australian Institute of Welfare Officers, the Congregational Union, and the Diabetes Federation of Australia.

There was also a massive increase in Associate members from 10 in 1970 to over 600 in 1975 emanating from a wide range of disciplines well beyond the social welfare sector.[6] ACOSS now described itself as "a broadly based independent association of social agencies, welfare consumer organizations, professional, employee and employer groups and individuals, drawn from all fields of social welfare in Australia".[7]

Leadership within ACOSS gradually switched from the old traditional charity elite to a wider group of welfare sector figures. Brotherhood of St Laurence social activist David Scott succeeded long-time New South Wales Council of Social Service representative Judith Green[8] as President in 1973, and actively encouraged ACOSS to become more involved in public policy debates.[9] Also influential were a younger group of ideological activists known as the "Young Turks", many of whom had been trained by Murray Geddes, a lecturer in Social Work at the University of New South Wales. This new generation of activists sought not only to pursue ideological objectives concerning wealth, redistribution and political decision-making, but also aimed to establish careers and influence for themselves.[10] According to Joan Brown, the "Young Turks had a passionate idealism that was worth harnessing to the work of ACOSS – though it was some-times necessary to insist on accuracy and ensure that their output was positive, not just polemical".[11]

Another significant change in ACOSS was the appointment of an over-seas person, Edward Pennington, to succeed Joan Brown as

Secretary-General in September 1974. Pennington had previously been the Executive Director of the Social Planning and Research Council (SPRC) of Hamilton and District in Canada, an organization which addressed similar issues to ACOSS.[12] Pennington's appointment was resented by some of the "Young Turks" who may have viewed his presence as a threat to their own career plans. A number of them actively sought to discredit Pennington in the eyes of the Commonwealth Government. The Directors of the State Councils of Social Service even used to caucus prior to ACOSS Board Meetings in an attempt to exclude Pennington from decision-making.[13]

Consumer Involvement

ACOSS made some efforts to consult with welfare consumers, and to organize them into a public political lobby. ACOSS welcomed the Council for the Single Mother and Her Child (CSMC) as a new consumer affiliate in 1971, and supported the CSMC's campaign to persuade the Commonwealth Government to amend the Social Services Act to include all unsupported mothers and their children.[14] ACOSS recognized its obligation to "assist users of social welfare services to make their views known".[15]

At the 1972 ACOSS National Conference, a number of speakers advocated greater consumer involvement in social service planning and delivery.[16] British guest speaker David Donnison stated: "We should give the spokesmen of our clients a say wherever there is an opportunity . . . That means of course that we have to start with the ACOSS Conference itself. There must be spokesmen of the consumers here and that means we have to think how to pay them, because they can't just come along and stay in Sydney hotels without help . . . No matter how hard we try as liberal minded progressive administrators of social programmes, we cannot speak for the clients. There is an inevitable and proper conflict between those who give out the benefits and those who receive them. Hence, those who receive them must be entitled to speak for themselves".[17] Similar views were expressed by South Australian academic Adam Jamrozik who called on the welfare sector to identify "ways and means that would enhance the political power of the recipients of welfare services and assure them of a legitimate political status".[18]

ACOSS ensured that consumer representatives participated in preparing ACOSS' evidence to the Poverty Inquiry and in writing the main part of the Report.[19] As part of this process, ACOSS initiated two anti-Poverty Conferences, one in New South Wales and one in South Australia, which were planned, organized and participated in by representatives of welfare consumer groups.[20] Consumer representatives also prepared a separate report for the Poverty Inquiry which was published under the title, *Are We Second Class Citizens?*[21]

ACOSS regularly criticized the absence of government recognition of, or structures for consultation with, welfare consumers. ACOSS acknowledged, however, that the level of consumer participation in the voluntary sector was also unsatisfactory, and urged welfare groups to provide resources and assistance to consumer groups.[22]

ACOSS did manage to secure some consumer representation within its own structures. For example, consumer groups such as the Australian Commonwealth Pensioners Federation and the National Council for the Single Mother and Her Child contributed to ACOSS publications. Similarly, a "small but significant" group of low-income representatives attended the eighth national ACOSS Conference held in May 1974.[23] A representative of one of these consumer groups – the CSMC – was invited to address the Conference.[24] However, some Aboriginal representatives walked out of the Conference in a protest against alleged tokenism.[25]

ACOSS canvassed plans to establish a national coalition of welfare consumers as a counterweight to professionally dominated services and interests,[26] but no such body emerged. Overall, the actual representation of consumers within ACOSS' structures remained limited and tentative.

ACOSS Objectives and Activities

ACOSS adopted an explicitly universalistic approach to welfare based on promoting human rights for all citizens, and the integration of social and economic concerns.[27] According to ACOSS, "Social welfare was no longer seen as primarily a gap-filling operation attending to emergency functions, and withdrawing when the regular social structures – the family, the economic system are again working properly". Instead, "social welfare is regarded as a proper legitimate function of modern industrial society in helping the individual achieve self fulfilment; it implies no stigma, no emergency, no abnormalcy".[28]

Nevertheless, at the same time, ACOSS' new Constitution (adopted in October 1972) emphasized "the carrying out of programmes designed to contribute to the elimination of poverty and the promotion of the well-being of disadvantaged and vulnerable individuals and groups".[29] That is, ACOSS continued primarily to espouse a welfarist model based on the elimination of poverty via incremental changes to social welfare spending, rather than a social justice model based on addressing the structural basis of inequality via a broader redistribution of income and wealth.

ACOSS' major involvement in the Poverty Inquiry was indicative of this dual concern with broader social policy goals, and a particular concentration on disadvantaged groups. ACOSS presented a 362 page submission to the Poverty Inquiry which defined poverty "as a life condition created by a constellation of deprivation factors which together result in a standard of living significantly below that acceptable for and by the community".[30]

ACOSS also outlined what it means to be in poverty: "Being poor in any society is to be undervalued, to be deprived of dignity and human rights and to be deprived of opportunities to realize your full potential. Being poor in an affluent society is to feel a sense of exclusion from those things which the rest of society take for granted, and which are constantly placed before you on radio and television as desirable and reasonable aspirations. It is to find that while middle and upper income groups have any number of opportunities to get the utmost out of their abilities, you and your children will be confronted with endless additional handicaps which will defeat all but the most determined".[31]

ACOSS suggested a 13-point attack on the income aspects of poverty in Australia. Recommended reforms included the establishment of a guaranteed income, adequate minimum wages, equal pay for women, pensions for all lone parents (including lone fathers), greater availability of superannuation, and a comprehensive income maintenance program for accident victims.[32]

ACOSS continually advocated for more adequate rates of social security benefits and pensions, and supported introduction of a guaranteed minimum income scheme to replace the existing social security payments system.[33] But they cautioned that financial assistance on its own would not eliminate poverty. Other forms of intervention around housing, health, education and employment would also be necessary to limit the incidence of poverty and disadvantage. ACOSS strongly opposed the abolition of the pensions means test, arguing that it would disadvantage lower income groups.

In addition to the more traditional concerns of the non-government welfare sector, ACOSS began to focus on a broader range of social policy issues. ACOSS concerns included the establishment of a national superannuation scheme that would ensure adequate provision for all aged persons, the establishment of a national compensation scheme that would provide compensation according to need rather than cause, a more progressive and equitable taxation system, expanded legal aid services, increased emphasis on the social and communal needs of migrants including greater accessibility to interpreters, and promoting the rights of tenants including the establishment of a new national forum on housing policy titled Shelter.

ACOSS also argued in favour of improved family planning services, higher quality family support services, improved consumer accessibility to government departments and services, removing discrimination against Aborigines, the right of all Australians to adequate health care via the introduction of a national health care scheme, expanded home help services for the chronically ill, improved services for the physically and mentally handicapped, more targeted assistance to industry, the principles of the new Family Law Bill, and the civil and political rights enshrined in the new Human Rights Bill.

Other activities included co-ordinating advice and support to the victims of Cyclone Tracy in Darwin, an evaluation of regional community development schemes as reflected in the Australian Assistance Plan, joint publication with ABSCHOL of a Directory of Agencies for Aboriginal Welfare, development of a foster care manual, a study of why children enter out of home care, promoting a social welfare manpower scheme, recommending establishment of a national council of social welfare education, undertaking a social planning study of two of the proposed new cities, and participation in conferences of the International Council on Social Welfare (ICSW). Joan Brown, for example, was elected both to the Asian Regional Executive and the International Executive of the ICSW. ACOSS also organized two biennial national welfare conferences in 1972 and 1974, and a national Family and Child Welfare Conference.

An Early Conservative Critic

ACOSS' increasing enthusiasm for universalistic social policy agendas provoked an early conservative critic. Paddy McGuiness, a former Private Secretary to the Social Security Minister, Bill Hayden, wrote in response to ACOSS' views on the proposed guaranteed minimum income scheme. McGuiness argued that ACOSS was ambivalent about the scheme because its successful introduction would push much of ACOSS' constituency – the welfare workers – out of work. In McGuiness' words: "As well as the poor, the social workers we shall have always with us".[34]

McGuiness' attack represented an early example of the application of public choice theory to the social welfare arena.[35] The implication of McGuiness' comment was that the welfare lobby is motivated by its own selfish career interests, rather than by a genuine concern for the poor and disadvantaged. In response, ACOSS Policy Officer Philippa Smith clarified that ACOSS did support a guaranteed minimum income scheme. However,

ACOSS believed that cash was insufficient on its own to eliminate poverty. Rather the poor also required access to child care, legal advice, labour market programs, and housing. Smith denied that ACOSS wished to retain the welfare system per se, or to defend the interests of social workers.[36]

Lobbying Strategies

ACOSS largely abandoned its traditional behind-the-scenes lobbying approach, and instead adopted a more assertive lobbying strategy based on "public statements and working to build community and media support for necessary change".[37]

However, this shift did not come about without some internal controversy. During a 1971 Executive Committee debate over health insurance, the New South Wales Council of Social Service representative argued that ACOSS "should not tell the Federal Government what to do". But others felt ACOSS had a right to critique government policies both prior to and following the passage of legislation. Internal dispute also occurred in relation to ACOSS' decision to seek involvement in national economic discussions with the government. A New South Wales representative opposed this proposal, arguing that ACOSS would be seen as a group with a "barrow to push". The Victorian Council of Social representative Walter Lippman responded that if ACOSS had no "barrow to push", there was no justification for existing. Lippman argued that ACOSS must push "welfare interests".[38]

Over time Lippman's view became dominant. For example, the campaign to promote ACOSS' submission to the 1975–76 Commonwealth Budget included a press release, telephone calls and letters to the media, letters to the editor, letters to the Prime Minister, the Treasurer and other Ministers, and the distribution of ACOSS' recommendations as widely as possible to the general community.[39] Similarly, ACOSS' campaign against the proposed abolition of the pensions means test included press releases, and the sending of a letter calling for a moratorium on further action to the Welfare Committee of Caucus, and to every member of Parliament.[40]

These public pressure tactics also contributed to ACOSS increasing its media profile. Joan Brown recalls ACOSS establishing "a good relationship with the media. We were a source of information and comment. There was press, radio and television coverage of our major meetings and some of our initiatives".[41] ACOSS' media coverage rose sharply in the last years of the Coalition Government. Between June 1971 and December 1972, for example, at least 35 references to ACOSS appeared in the daily press, many concerned with ACOSS' call for a national inquiry into social welfare.[42] Later there was substantial coverage of ACOSS' evidence to the Commonwealth Inquiry into Poverty.

ACOSS' relationship with the Commonwealth Government

ACOSS developed an active working relationship with both the Liberal/National Party Coalition and Australian Labor Party governments. Regular meetings were held with Coalition Ministers such as William Wentworth (Social Services), and with leading public servants from a range of portfolios (Immigration, Labour and National Service, Health, Social Services etc.).[43]

In an address to the 1972 ACOSS Annual General Meeting, the Director-General of the Department of Social Services Mr L. B. Hamilton stated: "The Department and its staff at all levels value very much the co-operation received from your Secretary-General. We are told things we ought to consider on the one hand and when we have got some problems of our own or when we want some help on the international scene it is given readily and willingly by your Secretary-General. The progress and real cooperation over the last six years has been striking".[44]

Nevertheless, there was also some tension within the relationship. In its 1971 pre-Budget submission, ACOSS strongly criticized the government's failure to increase social security payments. In response, the Secretary of the Department of Social Services reportedly phoned the ACOSS Chairperson, David Scott, and warned him that ACOSS' government funding could be threatened by its public criticism of government policies.[45]

ACOSS unsuccessfully sought representation in the government's annual economic consultations with industry and commerce. In a letter to the Prime Minister in May 1972, ACOSS (concerned at the impact government policies were having on the poor and unemployed) urged the need for consultations with the social welfare sector on the economy. The Prime Minister (apparently reflecting Treasury policy) said in reply that the government was unable to agree to ACOSS representation since participation in the consultations was limited to "those few nation-wide organizations of broad representation which are able to offer useful information on current trends and prospects in the major sectors of economic activity".[46] It was to be another ten years before ACOSS would gain access to pre-budget consultations with the Prime Minister and Cabinet.

ACOSS welcomed the election of the Whitlam Labor Party Government in December 1972, and generally supported government policies. For example, ACOSS praised the anti-poverty initiatives adopted by the Whitlam Government in its first few months as designed "to improve the position of the poor".[47] ACOSS also campaigned in favour of various government proposals including the Family Law Bill, Medibank, and the Compensation Bill.

ACOSS attained increased access to government during this period as reflected in meetings with senior public servants and government ministers such as Al Grassby (Immigration) and Bill Hayden (Social Security); the attendance of ministers at ACOSS functions; membership of government forums and advisory bodies such as the Immigration Advisory Council, the Social Welfare Commission's Working Party on Social Welfare Manpower, the Health Insurance Commission, and the Advisory Council for Social Security and Welfare; and a close relationship with the Social Welfare Commission around various policy initiatives.[48] The government also contracted ACOSS to undertake a number of consultations with the non-government sector including assisting welfare client groups to make submissions to the Henderson Poverty Inquiry.[49]

Overall, ACOSS appears to have been recognized by the government as a significant consultative and advisory body.[50] However, given the general ideological congruence between ACOSS' viewpoints and those of the government, it is difficult to segregate the extent of ACOSS' influence. Some commentators argue that ACOSS played a significant role in shaping government policy,[51] whilst others believe its direct influence on government policy may have been limited.[52]

Some key ACOSS objectives such as the introduction of the supporting mothers benefit, the upgrading of the B class widows to a standard A class rate for all widows, the establishment of a national housing forum, and the introduction of expanded interpreter services were introduced by the government.[53] Other initiatives such as the creation of the Australian Legal Aid Office and the introduction of Medicare may have reflected some ACOSS influence. But equally major ACOSS campaigns for introduction of a lone father's pension, the abolition of waiting periods for unemployment and sickness beneficiaries, and against the abolition of the means test for pensions were largely ignored by the government.

There was also some overt conflict. In part, this reflected continued tensions between government bureaucrats and the non-government welfare sector.[54] ACOSS was also critical of government policies which it believed failed to give particular priority to the needs of low-income earners. For example, ACOSS opposed the abolition of the means test for pensioners, and the abolition of the Social Welfare Commission.[55] These tensions came to the fore when the government reduced ACOSS' core funding grant in the

1975 Budget. This episode and the subsequent ACOSS campaign for increased funding is discussed in greater detail in chapter 6.

Funding

ACOSS' income continued to rise although so did costs and expenditure. In 1972, the Coalition Government gave ACOSS a major boost by agreeing to increase the international Grant from $5,000 to $10,000, and the ceiling of the matching grant from $20,000 to $40,000.[56] The Whitlam years saw a substantial increase in the Australian Government grant to ACOSS and the availability of project grants from the Social Welfare Commission and the Poverty Inquiry. ACOSS' income rose from $42,000 in 1970 to 175,000 in 1974, facilitating a substantial expansion of both staff and programs.

However, ACOSS' core grant was reduced to $90,000 in the 1975 Budget. The resulting ACOSS Action Campaign persuaded the government to provide an additional grant of $60,000. Despite this, ACOSS was still forced to make substantial cuts to staff and programs including the departure of Secretary-General Ed Pennington. By the time of Prime Minister Whitlam's sacking in November 1975, ACOSS faced grave financial difficulties.[57]

Case Study of Social Action: the Campaign for a National Welfare Inquiry

From 1970–1972, ACOSS campaigned for an independent national inquiry into social welfare and living conditions in Australia. This campaign reflected increasing public concern about the level of poverty and disadvantage in Australia. ACOSS pointed out that there had been no broadly based national review of social welfare since the 1940s, yet there had been enormous changes in community attitudes, welfare expenditure, service delivery and service structure since that time. ACOSS recommended an urgent re-examination of the values and goals of social security policies, the allocation of financial resources, the method of service delivery, and the appropriate division of responsibility between Commonwealth, State and local government and the voluntary sector.[58]

The May 1972 ACOSS report calling for a national welfare inquiry was launched in both Canberra and the various states. Copies of the report were circulated to members of the national and state parliaments, to all ACOSS members, and to the media.[59] Support for ACOSS' viewpoint was provided by the Anglican Archbishop of Sydney, Archbishop Loane, the Primate of the Anglican Church, the most Reverend Dr Frank Woods, 24 Anglican diocesan bishops, the Social Responsibilities Commission of the General Synod of the Church of England, and the Opposition Labor Party. A telegram signed by 45 community leaders, heads of churches and welfare agencies was sent to the Prime Minister calling for a welfare inquiry.[60] ACOSS also sought and received some support from State Ministers responsible for social welfare.[61] And the call for an inquiry was endorsed by a number of media outlets including editorials in *The Age*,[62] and *Sydney Morning Herald*.[63]

ACOSS' campaign appears to have exerted substantial influence on the Coalition Government's decision to establish a Commission of Inquiry into Poverty headed by Professor Ronald Henderson in September 1972. ACOSS welcomed the decision to establish the Poverty Inquiry, but argued that the inquiry should be extended to cover the whole area of social welfare.[64] According to ACOSS, "An inquiry into Poverty in the form now mooted by the government would be useful only if it is seen as one of a series of studies to be incorporated into a broad and comprehensive inquiry into social welfare. Poverty has much wider implications than cash benefits, it is related to the availability and accessibility of all services, including housing, health, welfare, legal aid and others".[65]

ACOSS' arguments appear subsequently to have influenced the Whitlam Government's decision to broaden the Commission of Inquiry into Poverty by the appointment of four additional commissioners concerned with law and poverty, selected economic issues, education and poverty, and medical/sociological aspects of poverty.[66] Nevertheless, the inquiry remained focused primarily on identifying remedial solutions to disadvantage, rather than addressing the structural causes of poverty and inequality.[67]

Questions for Discussion

➤ Consider some of the key factors that influenced ACOSS becoming a more vocal lobby group.

➤ Discuss ACOSS' relationship with users (consumers) of welfare services.

➤ Did ACOSS have any real influence on the direction of Australian social policy?

3

Watchdog for the Poor, 1976–1985

In contrast to the welfare expansion of the Whitlam Government years, the next decade found ACOSS operating in a relatively hostile political environment. Economic rationalism increasingly became the dominant influence on government policy. The Liberal/National Coalition Government led by Malcolm Fraser was at best unsympathetic to welfare spending and at worst ideologically opposed. The Australian Labor Party Government elected in 1983 also gave priority to economic over social concerns.

ACOSS responded to this adverse political climate by firmly establishing itself as the key lobby group of the non-government welfare sector. The ACOSS membership structure consisted of three categories: full members comprising about 40 national welfare organizations plus the eight State and Territory Councils of Social Service, other affiliated government and non-government social welfare organizations, and associate members.[1]

ACOSS claimed to represent "the voice of the seriously disadvantaged in the public and political arena",[2] and to embrace over 2,500 welfare organizations including traditional charitable service agencies, self-help and consumer groups, and professional organizations.[3]

Former ACOSS Secretary-General Colin Menzies clarified that ACOSS did not claim to represent the poor in any direct democracy sense, but rather to represent their broad political and economic interests: "One of the characteristics of the poor is that they are not organized. There are no viable unemployed people's organizations. A lot of the disenfranchised poor, their interests were represented by welfare agencies who dealt with them on a day-to-day basis and had some understanding of their problems. ACOSS' role was to articulate policy positions that advantaged poor people".[4]

In practice, ACOSS seems to have shifted during this period from its traditional dependence on the large charity organizations towards a greater engagement with the needs of the increasing number of small community-based organizations. According to long-term ACOSS activist Patricia Harper, the "community-based movement developed at least in part as a reaction to the inadequacies of the charitable organizations in adapting their services to the needs of clients . . . ACOSS then sought to reconcile these various strands, and to move away from representing simply the traditional residual perspective of the charities".[5] This process appears to have alienated some older and larger ACOSS affiliates.[6]

The retirement of David Scott as President in 1977 seems to have introduced a challenging period for ACOSS. To be sure the quality of ACOSS staff remained high with both Joan McLintock and Phillipa Smith making significant long-term contributions to ACOSS' productivity.[7] But organizationally ACOSS was plagued by factional disputes reflecting both ideological differences and personality, gender, and state-based divisions. These disputes tended to debilitate ACOSS, and to lessen its public credibility and effectiveness.

For example, one disagreement concerned the relative merits of universal payments versus selective payments.[8] The ACOSS Social Policy Officer Philippa Smith appears to have formed a view that ACOSS needed to "abandon universalism and embrace means-testing". However, this view was not always shared by the ACOSS Board. The dispute was also partly personality-based since Philippa Smith was an extremely successful publicist, and was regarded by some ACOSS officials as "getting too big for her boots". As a result, determination of policy on universalism and means testing was interpreted by many as a vote in favour of or against Philippa Smith.[9]

A further conflict involved the larger State Councils of Social Service and the smaller State Councils. The smaller states saw ACOSS as their avenue to information and influence whereas the larger Councils such as Victoria and New South Wales could basically run their own show. The Victorian Council of Social Service (VCOSS) even passed a motion to disaffiliate from ACOSS in 1980, although this was never implemented.[10]

The disputes manifested themselves both in conflict between ACOSS Boards and professional staff, in conflict between staff and in the selection of staff, and in conflict within the Board itself. For example, there was tension between the ACOSS Director Ian Yates and Philippa Smith during the mid-late 1970s over whether ACOSS should have a single advocate who was the acknowledged expert in the field, or alternatively be an organization with a single spokesperson who would represent a summation of all the views of the membership.[11]

Similarly, when Winston O'Reilly was defeated for the Presidency by

Murray Geddes in 1979, he set up a large Working Party on Proposition 16 (pertaining to the elimination of poverty) which acted as a virtual alternative or dissident ACOSS Board. As President, Geddes then tried to take over the role of public spokesperson for ACOSS which was resented by staff.[12] In 1982, Joan McLintock was awarded the position of Secretary-General over Chris Sidoti with the support of only half the ACOSS Board. Similarly, Bruce McKenzie was elected President of ACOSS in 1983 by only one vote over Alan Nichols. And the choice of Colin Menzies over Philippa Smith as Secretary-General in 1983 also caused much division, and led to the resignations of both Smith and McLintock.[13]

In 1985 a faction comprising Julian Disney, Merle Mitchell, Mark Lyons, Tony Lawson, and Patricia Harper sought and gained election to the key positions in ACOSS. The Disney group argued that ACOSS at that time had a low standing in the community, had lost its links with its membership, and had a very bad reputation within government. The larger Church-based agencies were allegedly indifferent or embarrassed at times. It was also alleged that the ACOSS Secretary General Colin Menzies had a capacity to alienate people, especially the Prime Minister.[14] In contrast, the Disney group promised to rebuild ACOSS at staff, Board and constituency level, regain credibility in its relationship with government, and strengthen its public profile.[15]

Whilst the views expressed by the Disney group are obviously subjective and the ousted Board and sacked Secretary General Colin Menzies may interpret events differently, the election of the new Board does appear to have lifted ACOSS' standing and effectiveness.

Consumer Involvement

ACOSS made significant efforts to involve consumer groups and representatives in its organizational structure, but these efforts seemed to yield few tangible results. Only a small number of consumer groups (e.g. the National Council for the Single Mother and Her Child, Association of Civilian Widows, Australian Pensioners Association, and Parents Without Partners) were able to directly influence ACOSS' decision-making process.

A number of initiatives were taken in an attempt to overcome both organizational and resource barriers to greater consumer involvement. A 1976 amendment to the ACOSS constitution committed the Council to "promoting citizen, consumer and community participation in social welfare activities, both government and non-government".[16] Three years later ACOSS allocated $1000 to enable low income, self-help and consumer groups to participate in ACOSS activity. ACOSS also played a key role in assisting the establishment of the Lone Parent Federation, and created an Australian Self-Help Network to give consumers increasing power over decision-making, resources and information.[17]

The 1981 ACOSS Congress passed a resolution calling on the Council "to place greater emphasis on assisting low-income and disadvantaged people to speak on their own behalf, rather than speaking for them . . . that ACOSS investigate ways of increasing the representation of low-income and disadvantaged people in its decision-making structures and that a report on this be prepared for Congress 1982. That in the meantime, the number of low-income people and/or consumers on ACOSS committees be immediately increased".[18] And the 1983 Congress called for Constitutional amendments to ensure direct consumer representation in ACOSS.[19]

Nevertheless, few consumer groups played a noticeable part in ACOSS activities. Whatever its intentions, ACOSS failed to develop effective community development strategies to engage with consumers.[20] A paper delivered at the 1979 ACOSS Congress by Judy Cassar (an ACOSS Board member representing the self-help Action and Resource Centre) seems to explain why consumers felt disenfranchised:

> The problem with ACOSS is that it is dominated by middle class professionals and social workers. They are people who work for and with low income people, but have not in the majority of cases been, and are not, low income people . . . Most low income people are effectively excluded from ACOSS. They are excluded because they cannot afford the cost of their participation, because of in-fighting and complex jargon, meeting procedures and hidden agendas . . . Many of the members of ACOSS are traditional welfare agencies. In helping low income people these traditional welfare agencies create dependency by doing everything for people and not letting them help themselves. It is not surprising that this protective paternalism is reflected in ACOSS programs and policies.[21]

ACOSS Objectives and Activities

ACOSS rejected the prevailing emphasis on public expenditure restraint to control inflation. ACOSS argued instead for more expansionary government policies designed to promote social and economic equity. ACOSS defined its role as that of a "democratic watchdog, pointing out and endeavouring to reverse those undemocratic aspects and destructive forces in our social structure which allow poverty and inequality to exist".[22]

ACOSS' number one priority was the struggle to reduce unemployment and protect the rights of the unemployed. ACOSS constantly criticized the government's failure to undertake significant action to reduce unemployment. Various statements and reports were issued identifying the social and individual costs of unemployment, promoting alternative policies such as job creation programs to assist the unemployed, countering bias against the unemployed, and advocating fairer eligibility criteria for receipt of unemployment benefits.

ACOSS also made the elimination of poverty a major priority, calling on the government to set specific targets and goals for the alleviation of poverty. In 1979, the ACOSS Congress passed Proposition 16 which declared that "ACOSS should mobilize people in Australia around the elimination of poverty, with all its resources marshalled around that aim". ACOSS urged the government to raise income security payments above the poverty line as soon as possible.[23] During the 1980 Federal election campaign, letters were sent to the leaders of the major political parties asking what action they planned to take on poverty.

ACOSS argued in favour of an expanded social security safety net that would protect people from falling below the poverty line, and campaigned successfully for the introduction of a lone parent pension. At the same time, ACOSS favoured the targeting of resources to those groups most in need, and argued that age pensions and family allowance payments should be means tested. Nevertheless, ACOSS refused to endorse the ALP Government's assets test on pensions, arguing that under the test fairness was considered only between those people receiving pensions and benefits, not between all Australians.

ACOSS urged the reform of Social Security law, administration and appeals procedures in order to avert possible injustices. ACOSS campaigned for the establishment of independent social security advice and advocacy services for low income people, and played a key role in the establishment of the New South Wales Welfare Rights Unit.

ACOSS favoured a more progressive and equitable tax system that would increase the amount of revenue available for support programs for low income earners. The Council seems to have played a significant role alongside the Australian Council of Trade Unions and women's and consumer groups in defeating the proposed consumption tax at the 1985 Tax Summit.[24] ACOSS claimed that the final position adopted by the Summit was "closer to where we started than it will be to the initial bargaining position of any other sector. There will be no regressive broad-based consumption tax. There will be more for those with children. Low income and poor people will be protected. Poverty traps will be reduced. Tax avoidance will be reduced".[25]

ACOSS devoted considerable resources to enhancing the operations of the non-government welfare sector. They established a Non-Government

Sector Welfare Committee to strengthen the role and identity of the sector, and to extend its ability to participate in government decisions affecting welfare programs. In addition, they created the Australian Non-Government Sector Tomorrow program which was designed to provide opportunities for non-government welfare organizations to come together to develop future planning and evaluation strategies.

Another initiative involved organizing a forum of the major national Non-Government Welfare Coordinating Bodies comprising ACOSS, the Australian Council on the Ageing, the Australian Council for Rehabilitation of the Disabled, the Australian Council for Overseas Aid, the Australian pre-School Association, and the National Youth Council of Australia. ACOSS also undertook a study of the non-government welfare sector in conjunction with the Social Welfare Research Centre.

ACOSS sought to improve and expand its relations with the business sector. The aim was both to influence the policies of what was viewed as a powerful lobby group, and to secure finance from a potential funding source. In April 1980, ACOSS organized a series of seminars on the "Social Responsibilities of Business". The seminars aimed at promoting dialogue between business and welfare organizations on social issues, and enabling business to be more aware of the work and interests of ACOSS. ACOSS argued that "business, in addition to its traditional role of doing well, should also now be doing good".[26]

Following these seminars, ACOSS succeeded in developing a Corporate Associates Program comprising 16 major companies interested in corporate philanthropy. However, tensions remained between ACOSS and the business sector as reflected in policy disagreements at the 1985 National Tax Summit.[27]

Other ACOSS priorities included the retention of legal aid as a national service, the promotion of a multicultural society and a fair and humanitarian immigration policy, greater access for the poor to finance and credit, the expansion of public housing to meet the needs of low income earners, opposing discrimination against Aborigines and supporting their claim for land rights, and promoting Australian involvement in the International Council on Social Welfare (ICSW) including the hosting of the 1979 ICSW Regional Conference in Melbourne.

ACOSS also recommended the establishment of a universal system of health care funded by an income tax levy and welcomed the introduction of Medicare, argued that aged care funding should give preference to domiciliary care to promote the independence of the elderly rather than institutional care, supported a flexible retirement age offering optimum freedom of choice within a particular age range, campaigned for an effective Freedom of Information Bill so that the rationale for government programs could be adjudged and evaluated by the people most affected by them, emphasized the need for effective human rights legislation, recommended that emergency relief requirements be met directly by the Department of Social Security, claimed that evaluation of welfare programs could help to provide for a more efficient use of available resources, and commented critically on the 1976 Bailey Report which recommended the devolution of Commonwealth welfare/health programs to the States.

Ideology

ACOSS gradually moved away from its traditional welfarist emphasis on minor increases in particular social security programs, and instead adopted a broader structural focus on income redistribution. Social and economic inequality was to be addressed by reforms in taxation and a number of other policy areas such as health, housing, and education.[28]

This shift can be formally traced to the adoption of Proposition 16 on the elimination of poverty in September 1979. Proposition 16 committed ACOSS to reforming "unequal structures and distribution of power in the community".[29] According to Chris Sidoti, Proposition 16 meant that ACOSS would no longer argue for welfarist $2 increases in various pensions and benefits, but would instead argue for "justice and equity".[30] Nevertheless, many of the specific recommendations emanating from Proposition 16 still refer to minor welfarist increases in social security payments.[31]

It was only later that ACOSS began to emphasize macro-economic issues (the size of the total welfare budget as a percentage of Gross National Product) as opposed to micro issues (the dollar increase in a particular line item of the welfare budget).[32] For example, ACOSS' submission to the 1983 National Economic Summit was titled *Distribution in Recession* both to underline a commitment to income redistribution as the only way to achieve a just and more equitable society, and to symbolize an end to the concept of welfare as merely peripheral assistance to the poor.[33]

Criticisms from Right and Left

ACOSS' advocacy of higher government spending and greater government intervention led to criticism from some conservative groups and commentators.

Conservative journalist Greg Sheridan, for example, criticized the Federal Government for funding leftist lobby groups such as ACOSS that advocated greater government spending on welfare.[34] Similarly, the conservative journal *Newsweekly* criticized ACOSS for allegedly "moving away from its object of helping the disadvantaged into the province of political action, which appears to further the interests of welfare professionals rather than the poor and underprivileged".[35]

Further conservative criticism focused on ACOSS' funding arrangement with sections of the corporate sector. Journalist Bob Browning argued that the legitimacy of business and free enterprise was being undermined by "New Class" welfarist groups such as ACOSS.[36] And both the *Australian Financial* Review and the neo-liberal think tank, the Institute of Public Affairs, slammed ACOSS for favouring income redistribution.[37]

All these critics seemed to be influenced by the assumption that welfare groups should stick to providing direct charitable services for the poor and underprivileged, and avoid comment on public policy debates. In response, ACOSS argued that governments were obligated in a democratic society to provide disadvantaged minority groups with the "resources, as well as the freedom, to argue their interests alongside more powerful groups".[38]

ACOSS also received criticism from left-wing sources who claimed that ACOSS was wedded to a "liberal political stance" which identified poverty as a "social problem" that could be cured by better social planning and the promotion of community development strategies, rather than recognizing that poverty was "an endemic aspect of capitalism".[39] ACOSS was censured for allegedly cooperating with the conservative policies of the Liberal-National Coalition Government, and for refusing to enter into coalitions with the labour movement.[40] Criticism was also levelled at ACOSS' belief in the relative benevolence and potential social responsibility of big business.[41] It was argued that instead of seeking a redistribution of wealth within the existing capitalist system, ACOSS should be mounting a fundamental challenge to the prevailing political order.[42]

These progressive criticisms have some legitimacy in that ACOSS did continue to argue for minor increases in social security payments, rather than concentrating on broader structural inequalities in the economic system. ACOSS also seemed to place a naïve faith in the ability of groups with differing economic and political interests such as the Coalition Government, the union movement and the business sector to work together to achieve better outcomes for the poor and disadvantaged.

Nevertheless, over time ACOSS did begin to tackle the structural causes of poverty and inequality, and to advocate a broader redistribution of income via the taxation and economic systems.

Lobbying Strategies

ACOSS operated as an "insider" lobby group utilizing primarily strategies of cooperation and persuasion to promote change, although occasionally contest strategies were employed. ACOSS strategies included submissions to and meetings with government ministers, public seminars and campaigns, alliances with like-minded groups, addresses to conferences, media action, and research.

In an attempt to influence the broader economic debate, ACOSS began to produce its annual Budget proposals in a more sophisticated fashion. ACOSS moved away from the old "shopping list" of demands for extra welfare spending in every conceivable area which assumed an ever-increasing rise in welfare spending. Instead, ACOSS adopted economically literate proposals which identified or targeted key welfare priorities, and potential savings and possible new revenue sources such as broadening the taxation base.[43] For example, the 1979 ACOSS Budget Submission identified potential savings within the Social Security Budget that could be used to fund new programs. ACOSS also suggested additional sources of revenue such as higher taxation rates for high income earners, introduction of a capital gains tax, and a crackdown on tax evasion.[44]

ACOSS also compiled detailed information on the facts of welfare expenditure in an attempt to influence media coverage and public opinion. For example, in response to the growing public hostility to taxation and public sector expenditure, ACOSS published material explaining and justifying the substantial and growing expenditure on welfare as associated with wider economic, demographic and social changes.[45]

ACOSS developed a number of broad alliances and coalitions to support its objectives. For example, ACOSS worked closely with the "Share the Health Group", a coalition of community health groups seeking to raise awareness of the inequities and inadequacies of the health insurance system. Later ACOSS participated in the Defend and Extend Medicare Committee, a group created by a number of unions and community groups in Sydney to defend Medicare in the face of criticism from some sections of the medical profession. Another coalition involved the Fair Share campaign led by church-based welfare groups which aimed to bring all Australians above the poverty line.[46] ACOSS also utilized broad alliances during its invalid pension campaign as discussed in the case study below.

ACOSS employed a pro-active media strategy in order to facilitate media coverage. ACOSS Policy Officer Philippa Smith contributed a weekly column to the *Sun Herald* entitled "Social Security and You", published a number of feature articles in *The Bulletin*, and also received regular radio coverage. In addition, a number of ACOSS campaigns concerning the rights of the unemployed, poverty, human rights legislation, and invalid pensions attracted significant media interest.[47] According to Smith, "ACOSS became more aware that by creating a media profile and debate on welfare issues we placed pressure on the government for action to be taken".[48]

ACOSS' relationship with the Commonwealth Government

ACOSS' relationship with the Liberal-National Coalition Government from 1975–83 was characterized by a critical and often confrontationalist rejection of government policies. ACOSS saw its role as one of pressuring an ideologically unsympathetic government to adopt different policies that were more favourable to the interests of low income earners. The government in turn resented ACOSS' constant criticism and its perceived failure to grant equivalent praise to government initiatives which it supported.

Nevertheless, the Coalition Government recognized ACOSS as the senior umbrella non-government welfare organization, and granted the Council substantial access to key policy-makers. ACOSS held regular meetings with senior public servants, and with key ministers including the Treasurer John Howard. Leading government figures attended ACOSS meetings and seminars, and ACOSS was represented on a number of government forums and advisory bodies pertaining to social welfare, family law, industry assistance, legal aid, health services, disability, child care, and refugees. ACOSS was also included for the first ever time in 1982 in pre-budget discussions with the Prime Minister and Cabinet.[49]

ACOSS' impact on government policy appears to have been limited given that the minister and the government relied primarily on advice from the Department of Social Security's policy and research officers.[50] However, another former Department of Social Security analyst David Stanton recalls that ACOSS' credibility and influence improved substantially during this period: "They became more effective and got more access to Ministers for Social Security. Their sophistication grew in terms of their ability to define properly the cost and the likely impact of social policy measures they were advocating. So instead of just seeking improvements for the unemployed, they were able to define in quite concrete terms what they wanted to see and develop in the context of an overall budget strategy".[51]

ACOSS appears to have achieved some of its key policy objectives including the liberalization of invalid pension eligibility criteria, the introduction of welfare rights centres in Sydney, Canberra and Hobart, the passage of an effective Freedom of Information Bill, and the establishment of an Administrative Appeal Tribunal for social security appeals. Nevertheless, many of ACOSS' key recommendations concerning unemployment, poverty and social security payments were not successful.[52]

ACOSS initially developed a fairly harmonious relationship with the Australian Labor Party Government elected in March 1983. ACOSS sought to cooperate with the government to pursue what they assumed was the common objective of social justice. ACOSS appeared to be given unprecedented access to government as reflected in its involvement (as the only human services group) in the 1983 National Economic Summit, and its inclusion in the Economic Planning Advisory Council (EPAC) which was to act as the government's main advisory body on economic issues.

ACOSS argued that its involvement in EPAC gave it greater access to information and key policy makers, and provided formal government recognition of the role and legitimacy of the community sector. In short, ACOSS was included as the "fourth estate" to the triumvirate of government, business and unions.[53] However, some commentators argue that inclusion in these corporatist-style forums limited rather than enhanced ACOSS' public impact.[54]

Other indications of ACOSS' growing legitimacy included regular meetings with leading Ministers and public servants, the presence of leading government figures including Prime Minister Bob Hawke at ACOSS Congresses, and the funding of the Council to undertake a national consultation with pensioner groups on the proposed Assets Test of pensioners.

Nevertheless as 1983–84 progressed, ACOSS became more critical of the ALP Government. Criticisms related to the slow pace of reform and the failure of the government to implement a redistribution of wealth and income.[55] ACOSS also complained that peak business and union groups were being granted exclusive contact with the government at the expense of the community welfare sector. However, this public dissent seems to have had little impact on changing government policy which led ACOSS President Bruce McKenzie to complain that the Council was relatively powerless: "What power does ACOSS really have? It can't threaten the government with a strike. It is powerless. This is typical of people in poverty. When it comes to the crunch and you have to use muscle, we haven't got any".[56]

Conflict between ACOSS and the government became public in May 1984 when ACOSS refused to endorse the Economic Planning Advisory Council (EPAC) consensus that tax cuts should go to those with incomes over $30,000 per annum. ACOSS said that to give tax cuts to 95 per cent of taxpayers would be "a sell out on redistribution and economic justice".[57]

ACOSS also refused to endorse EPAC's statement that "the economy in all significant aspects was superior to the expectations of any group at the time of the Economic Summit" on the grounds that the lot of three million pensioners and beneficiaries had not improved.[58]

ACOSS' criticism provoked a vigorous response from the Prime Minister and the Treasurer which is discussed in greater detail in chapter 6. ACOSS responded by defending their right to express views contrary to those of the government. Whilst denying that it intended to be "confrontationalist", ACOSS argued that "on occasions its advocacy was more effective when conducted in public than in the corridors of power".[59]

Despite their differences of opinion with the government, ACOSS officially endorsed the ALP in the December 1984 election as the only party "offering any immediate hope to the unemployed, pensioner and disadvantaged person".[60] ACOSS also appointed a liaison officer in Canberra, and made long-term plans to shift its office to Canberra in order to improve communication channels with the government, although that plan was later shelved. The election of a new pragmatic ACOSS leadership in late 1985 seems to have contributed to improved relations with the government.

Funding

ACOSS experienced severe financial difficulties during the Fraser Government years which it attributed to the decreasing value of Commonwealth Government assistance. These financial difficulties arguably constrained ACOSS' ability to effectively pursue its policy objectives. In 1979, for example, the ACOSS Treasurer stated pessimistically that ACOSS could not survive another year without "substantially increased financial support".[61] In order to relieve the situation, ACOSS Secretary-General Ian Yates was forced to take six months leave without pay from November 1980 to May 1981.[62]

Subsequently ACOSS released a study which claimed substantial erosion of the real value of Commonwealth Government grants to over 65 per cent of voluntary welfare bodies since 1975. ACOSS argued that the government's expressions of support for the role played by the non-government welfare sector should be matched by financial support to enable agencies to meet the increasing demands being made upon them.[63]

ACOSS' financial situation improved somewhat in 1982 as a result of an increase in the overall government grant and extra funding for several major projects. The incoming Labor Government then further increased ACOSS' annual grant from $185,000 to $210,000.

Case Study of Social Action:
The Invalid Pension Campaign

During 1980 ACOSS received information concerning the tightening of eligibility criteria for invalid pensions which allegedly resulted in a number of severely disabled persons being taken off or refused the pension. ACOSS joined with a number of organizations representing disabled persons, lawyers, social workers, and doctors to mount a vigorous public campaign against the pensions crackdown.[64]

The coalition disseminated factual information on the treatment of individual pensioners by way of 200 case studies which indicated drastic changes to previous procedures, and other information from statistics and Department of Social Security guidelines. In addition, protest letters were sent to the Minister of Social Security and the Prime Minister, support was attained from State Ministers and organizations, and the concerns were heavily publicized in the media. At one stage the *Sydney Morning Herald* carried almost daily stories on people who had been taken off the invalid pension. [65]ACOSS and the Redfern Legal Centre also threatened to mount a legal challenge to the Department's new eligibility criteria.[66]

In December 1980, ACOSS and a number of pensioner groups jointly organized a public seminar entitled "Invalid Pensions: Rights and Wrongs". The then Social Security Minister Fred Chaney recalls being invited to participate in the seminar, and being greeted by "cameras from every TV station, lots of radio stations and reporters and a row of people in wheelchairs". According to Chaney, ACOSS "played the game hard", and engaged in some "strong emotional campaigning".[67]

Following the seminar, ACOSS and other organizations met with the Social Security Minister and Departmental representatives in a series of meetings and negotiated substantial changes to the invalid pension regulations and procedures that met most of ACOSS' concerns. For example, the new guidelines introduced in May 1981 re-emphasized the importance of social factors such as age, sex, education, and lack of relevant skills in determining eligibility for invalid pensions.[68]

But later ACOSS expressed concern that the guidelines were not being effectively implemented, and many thousands of pensioners were still being refused or taken off the pension. ACOSS held further negotiations with the Social Security Minister concerning the need for a new form and administrative procedures within the Department, the need to provide information to claimants and simpler wording of the guidelines, advice and assistance services, and quicker appeal procedures.[69]

ACOSS and allied groups subsequently held a phone-in in late 1982 which led to further concern over the sharp fall in the number of invalid pension beneficiaries. The results of the phone-in were published in a report titled *Unfit for the Pension* which documented the alleged "intolerance and bureaucratic insensitivity meted out" to many invalid pension claimants.[70] Subsequent ACOSS recommendations were included in the 1982 Budget including new transition proposals for invalid pensioners which allowed those pensioners entering the workforce to retain Health Care Card cover for 12 months without an income test. There would also be special arrangements for them to reapply for a pension during that time if they were unable to continue working.[71]

Questions for Discussion

➤ Discuss the impact of ACOSS' internal conflicts on their operations and effectiveness.

➤ How significant were the changes in ACOSS' ideological viewpoint? Were the criticisms from Left or Right groups justified?

➤ What factors influenced ACOSS' relationship respectively with Coalition and Labor Governments?

4

A Political Insider,
1985–1996

The long-term governance by the Australian Labor Party presented new challenges and opportunities for ACOSS. On the one hand, the government's adoption of an economic rationalist free market agenda narrowed the parameters of political debate. On the other hand, the government sought within this framework to target more resources to those welfare recipients who were in greatest need. In addition, the government established new corporatist-style structures to facilitate the inclusion of accepted interest groups such as ACOSS within their policy networks.[1]

ACOSS responded to this fluid political climate by adopting a more pragmatic and arguably more sophisticated political strategy aimed at ensuring a recognized role for the community welfare sector in national policy making. ACOSS emphasized its right to comment on all matters of public policy including the economy, rather than being solely limited to debating issues of income security. In doing so, ACOSS subtly highlighted its concern with the national interest as well as the narrower agendas of its own constituency.[2]

Whilst continuing to criticize government policies that harmed low income earners, ACOSS attempted to engage and challenge the government from within its defined economic rationalist parameters. In practice, ACOSS balanced its criticisms of government policy by publicly praising those measures with which it was in agreement. As a result, relations between ACOSS and the ALP Government underwent significant improvement. This improved relationship contributed to ACOSS' influence on government. In addition, ACOSS significantly increased its public and media profile, and gained general recognition as an important and effective lobby group.

ACOSS' effectiveness was enhanced by its internal stability, unity and membership growth. Consecutive Presidents Julian Disney, Merle Mitchell, and Robert Fitzgerald achieved high public and media profiles, acted as effective policy advocates, and maintained good relations with the broader ACOSS constituency. The paid Directors Mark Lyons, Garth Noweland-Foreman, and Betty Hounslow also made significant contributions to ACOSS' public credibility. And there was a significant increase in the number of national member organizations and affiliates from only 40 in 1987 to 62 in 1996, plus a jump to almost 300 associate members.

Consumer Involvement

The representation of welfare recipient and self-help groups within ACOSS remained an issue of contention. To be sure, constitutional amendments guaranteed the participation of the major national low income consumer groups such as the Civilian Widows Association, the Council for the Single Mother and Her Child and the Australian Pensioners Federation within the ACOSS Board. ACOSS also ensured that these groups were consulted on major policy issues such as the Social Security Review, and regularly involved them in delegations to government.[3] In addition, the early 1990s saw ACOSS co-opt a Senior Indigenous leader to their Board.

However, at other times ACOSS' claim to speak on behalf of low income groups was at best questionable. This was particularly the case with the unemployed given their lack of representation within ACOSS. For example, ACOSS' qualified support for the NewStart scheme for the unemployed was publicly challenged by the Tasmanian Unemployed Workers Union (UWU).

According to the UWU's coordinator, Bill Bartlett, "ACOSS has very cleverly manouvered itself into position as the number one voice of the poor and downtrodden, but who does it really represent? Not the unemployed obviously. The Unemployed Workers Union has never been involved, and never will be. ACOSS actually has as its main constituency charitable organizations such as the Salvation Army, St Vincent De Paul Society, etc. Many of these are directly involved in Federally funded training schemes for the unemployed. So in many cases the interests of ACOSS' constituent organizations are in direct conflict with the interests of the people the public face of ACOSS claim to represent".[4]

In response, the ACOSS Director Garth Noweland-Foreman claimed that there were "more low-income consumer representatives on the ACOSS Board than there are people associated with major charitable agencies". Noweland-Foreman also suggested that ACOSS' democratic structures provided ample opportunity for all community welfare groups to contribute to and influence ACOSS policies.[5]

ACOSS Objectives and Activities

ACOSS questioned the direction of government economic policy, rejecting the view held by government and the media that Australia was a high-taxed, high-spending country. Whilst accepting the need for some fiscal restraint, ACOSS criticized the Labor Government's excessive financial deregulation, harsh monetary policy including the reliance on high interest rates to slow import consumption, heavy cuts to public expenditure, and refusal to consider alternative fiscal measures such as higher taxation. ACOSS would later claim (with some validity) that if the government had listened to and acted on these concerns the severe recession of 1990–92 may not have occurred.[6]

ACOSS argued that economic rationalist policies imposed the heaviest sacrifice on social welfare recipients and disadvantaged users of community services. Instead, they urged increased investment in public infrastructure to encourage economic development and boost employment, and greater support for export industries to help companies become internationally competitive, strengthen trade links with Asia, and resolve Australia's balance of payments problems. ACOSS suggested that living standards were affected by access to community services and facilities and employment and educational opportunities in the immediate locality and region where people live – the spatial dimensions of equity – and established an Urban and Regional Development Unit to investigate major problems arising from local disadvantage.

ACOSS argued in favour of a more progressive and equitable tax system that would reverse the sharply declining level of tax revenue, and provide increased funds for support programs for low income earners. This meant opposing tax cuts for high income earners, rejecting proposals for a consumption tax and opposing the introduction or extension of other indirect taxes, recommending the reform of superannuation tax concessions to reduce their bias towards high income earners, and urging the removal of major business tax loopholes and distortions. ACOSS argued that these loopholes deprived the government of badly needed revenue, and encouraged business practices such as financial speculation and short-term profit making rather than longer-term productive investment, which aggravated Australia's economic problems.[7]

ACOSS aimed to promote full employment, provide more adequate and effective support for long-term jobless people and redress inequalities in both the education system and the labour market.[8] In response to the sharp rise in unemployment associated with the 1990–92 recession, ACOSS advocated policies designed both to alleviate the hardship being experienced by unemployed people, and to improve longer term job prospects. Particular attention was placed on expanding labour market programs. Later ACOSS recommended the introduction of a jobs development levy to fund existing and new initiatives to reduce unemployment and assist unemployed people. ACOSS also established a Future of Work Commission to examine the implications of the changing patterns of paid and unpaid work, and the contemporary meaning of the objective of full employment.

ACOSS favoured the elimination of poverty, and the establishment of an income security system which is fair, adequate and sustainable. ACOSS advocated increased rates of payment for particularly disadvantaged groups such as sole parents, the single adult unemployed, and young people, and campaigned specifically along with the State Councils of Social Service and the Brotherhood of St. Laurence for measures to reduce the high level of child poverty in Australia. ACOSS also opposed government attempts to cut or reduce the rights or entitlements of social security beneficiaries, and strongly rejected the government's proposed Work for the Dole scheme.

ACOSS was active in organizing community consultations around the Social Security Review, and generally supported the direction adopted in the Review papers including the proposals for a more active social security system. However, ACOSS was critical of some of the elements of compulsion in the NewStart package for the long-term unemployed, and the rehabilitation programs for the disabled. ACOSS also argued for a retirement income policy that would give improved levels of basic income support to those old age pensioners who are in greatest need, and supported the introduction of the national Child Support Scheme as a means of raising the living standards of children in sole-parent families.

A further ACOSS priority was the provision of efficient and quality health care accessible to all Australians. This included documenting the relationship between social inequality and poor health, emphasizing the continued importance of Medicare for low income earners, opposing changes that would increase the role of private health insurance, urging increased support for people with mental illness, and campaigning jointly with the Consumers Health Forum for the introduction of a national dental health scheme.

Other ACOSS priorities included a large increase in the Commonwealth Government's Financial Assistance Grants to the States to help finance education, health and other state community services, improved access to adequate and affordable housing including a benchmark that low income families should not spend more than 30 per cent of their income on housing costs, and specific strategies to address youth homelessness. ACOSS also recommended improved access to affordable justice, claimed that privatization might adversely impact on low income earners, established a Rural Issues Committee to monitor the specific issues in rural Australia that generate and alleviate poverty including transport costs, and aimed to gain for community services a recognition of their contribution to the social and economic wellbeing of individuals, families and communities.

In addition, ACOSS attempted to draw linkages between increased demands for emergency relief and the inadequacies of social security payments, recommended expanded child care services to assist the workforce participation of parents[9], sought to establish closer relations with the business community whilst simultaneously criticizing many of their economic activities and core beliefs, urged improved support services for migrants and refugees and a balance to be struck between family reunion and skilled and business migration, supported reforms to promote higher household savings, argued in favour of phone concessions for unemployed people, offered qualified support for the proposed Multi-Function Polis the city of the future planned for Adelaide, consistently supported moves towards self-determination for Aborigines including the 1993 Mabo judgement on native title and strongly supported the national inquiry into the Stolen Generation of Aboriginal children, opposed the imposition of bank charges on low income customers, rejected surrogacy arrangements, and condemned the introduction of mandatory sentencing legislation for juvenile offenders in Western Australia.

ACOSS played an important role in coordinating the activities of the non-government welfare sector. They organized sector consultations around the 1994 Industry Commission Inquiry into Charitable Organizations, and subsequently welcomed some of the key recommendations of the Inquiry pertaining to funding agreements and accountability arrangements and standards whilst rejecting other proposals relating to competition and benchmarking. ACOSS convened meetings of the Forum of Non-government Welfare Coordinating Bodies, and continued to participate in international social welfare particularly through membership of the International Council on Social Welfare and via active involvement alongside the Australian Council for Overseas Aid in the 1995 United Nations World Summit for Social Development. ACOSS also undertook a joint study tour of New Zealand, with the Australian Council of Trade Unions and the Australian Manufacturing Workers Union, to examine its experience of structural adjustment and social change.

Ideology

ACOSS espoused a social democratic view of the world which not only addressed the structural causes of poverty and inequality, but also went beyond the traditionally narrow agenda of the welfare sector to concern itself with the general health of the economy. According to ACOSS, they were concerned with "the way our economy generates and distributes resources, especially incomes policies and the tax/transfer system".[10]

ACOSS activist John Freeland called this new approach a movement from "the politics of redistribution" towards "the politics of distribution".[11] He argued that ACOSS was forced by its inclusion in key advisory bodies such as the Economic Planning Advisory Council to develop a more sophisticated macro-economic analysis. This meant participating in debates over wages policy and income distribution, and talking in terms of budget revenue, expenditure and deficits, the balance of payments and the terms of trade, and industry policy and employment generation, instead of merely seeking redistribution via the Department of Social Security.[12] For example, ACOSS played an active role in the business taxation debate because "too easy a life for business can mean less government revenue to support pensions and services".[13]

In general, ACOSS spoke of the need to promote both economic restructuring and social justice on the basis that they would complement each other. Social justice was necessary to provide the human resources, infrastructure and community cohesion which are essential to sustainable economic development. Economic restructuring was essential to produce the financial resources and jobs necessary to enhance social justice.[14]

Ideological Critics of ACOSS

ACOSS' pragmatic social democratic approach attracted criticism from both the Left and Right of the spectrum. Those with left-wing views argued that by accepting the government's economic rationalist agenda, ACOSS had dropped its traditional commitment to redistribution of income and a fairer distribution of wealth.

For example, prominent sociologist Lois Bryson argued that ACOSS had "abandoned the defence of broader and more progressive principles, and was now reduced to arguing only over 'how much' within the framework set by government".[15] Similarly social policy academic Sheila Shaver criticized an allegedly "defensive welfare lobby" for "increasingly couching its arguments within the parameters of economic rationalism".[16] And feminist Eva Cox accused ACOSS of "taking positions on the edges of the present economic rationalist model as supplicants asking for more compassion". According to Cox, by doing so, ACOSS had helped legitimize the prevailing economic rationalist orthodoxy.[17]

Some of these criticisms have legitimacy in that ACOSS did narrow its critique during this period to the government's specific priorities, rather than rejecting the government's overall economic rationalist model. Nevertheless, it is highly likely that stronger criticism of the government's overall agenda would have led to ACOSS' political marginalization as it did with those groups on the political Left who rejected the government's accord with the union movement.

ACOSS' activities also provoked criticism from neo-liberal sources who resented ACOSS' calls for increased government spending and higher taxation in order to reduce poverty.

For example, following Liberal Party leader John Hewson's controversial attack on ACOSS in October 1991,[18] a number of right-wing media commentators rushed to his defence. Journalist Paddy McGuiness accused ACOSS of espousing policies which increased, rather than decreased poverty and inequality. He claimed that ACOSS' call for higher welfare benefits without considering how they would affect the behaviour of recipients would damage the poor whilst benefiting people who do not need or deserve help.[19]

Similarly, former National Party Senator John Stone claimed that ACOSS "contained a significant number of denizens of the New Class who have parlayed their volubly expressed compassion into various forms of personal advancement, increased income, more comfortable lifestyles and so on. Their chief activity is not directed to, for example, the relief of poverty, but to devising various more or less complex programmes which they or their industry colleagues then administer to the greater good of the smaller number". According to Stone, many ACOSS proposals would "simply result in more poverty, or other forms of personal dependency by their clients, not less".[20]

Other harsh conservative critics of ACOSS included Sydney Institute Director Gerard Henderson, Institute of Public Affairs Senior Fellow Des Moore, and journalists Frank Devine, Paul Gray and Bob Browning.[21] Most of these critics appear to be inspired by public choice theory which holds that private rather than public provision of services is always preferable. Their attack on the welfare lobby seems to reflect a concern to defend the vested interests of the powerful and the wealthy, rather than any informed critique of the welfare sector or system.[22]

Lobbying Strategies

ACOSS defined its key lobbying targets as government at both the political and administrative levels, other key opinion leaders and interest groups such as media, business and unions, and general public opinion.[23] ACOSS employed a range of strategies to influence government policies including meetings with government ministers, staffers and ALP policy committees, submissions, publications, appearances at Senate inquiries and hearings, public pressure campaigns, public addresses to major forums, alliances with broader networks such as churches, unions, and community organizations, and use of the media.[24]

ACOSS claimed that the quality of its research and publications, and its economic analysis were key contributors to its lobbying success. According to former ACOSS President Julian Disney, ACOSS provided "detailed, meticulous, reasonable submissions. I'm dead against the ambit claim. This contributed to the degree of respect we got".[25] Similarly Sydney Morning Herald journalist Milton Cockburn noted that Disney "is a pragmatist who taught ACOSS the value of compromise, of giving kudos where it is due, so that its criticisms had a lot more credibility and hurt just a little bit more".[26]

ACOSS made a conscious decision to accept the government's economic framework including the need for continued restraint on the Budget deficit, and to argue its case within the parameters of that framework.[27] An explanation of this strategy was provided by ACOSS Director Mark Lyons in 1988. Lyons noted the importance of putting the welfare case in the language of economics, which was the dominant language in government as well as in business and the union movement. According to Lyons, ACOSS was able to argue that particular actions to reduce poverty would be neutral, or even positive in their economic impact – that is, would increase rather than diminish the efficiency and productivity of the economy. ACOSS was also able to demonstrate where additional revenue to finance additional social expenditure could be found, and to identify areas where expenditure could be cut.[28]

ACOSS formed a number of alliances in an attempt to increase its lobbying strength. ACOSS successfully utilized its links with the churches in its 1987 campaign against child poverty.[29] In 1993, ACOSS joined with eight other national peak bodies representing ethnic, women, overseas aid, union, environmental and Aboriginal groups to launch the New Visions forum calling for a more equitable society. ACOSS also cooperated with the minor political parties such as the Democrats and the Greens, and other lobby groups such as the Australian Conservation Foundation, the Australian

Federation of Consumer Organizations, the Australian Local Government Association, the Women's Electoral Lobby, and the Consumers Telecommunications Network on issues such as superannuation, environmental taxes, and communications services.[30]

In addition, ACOSS undertook a number of lobbying and public pressure campaigns. These included a 1986 campaign against Budget cuts to welfare expenditure involving advertisements in the major metropolitan daily newspaper in every state[31], organizing and funding a large group of sole parents to visit Canberra to protest changes announced by the government in the May 1987 Economic Statement, and the 1992 Day of Action on Unemployment.

ACOSS attained significantly greater media coverage during this period which was viewed as crucial for influencing policy makers and processes. The print media automatically contacted ACOSS for comments on all important policy debates, not only those relating to specifically welfare issues as had been the case in the past. ACOSS contributed to this improved relationship by appointing a journalist as publications and media liaison officer, and devoting considerable attention to developing a high media profile.

According to the first ACOSS media officer, Adam Farrar, the process of promoting a relationship with the media started from scratch: "I was part-time three days a week editing *Impact* and doing media liaison. I had two tasks. One was to turn *Impact* into a kind of journal which was credible – not a newsletter, but a news magazine in the welfare sector – and to use it to create a profile with the media. The second strategy was to make sure Julian Disney as the organizational performer became directly known to the Canberra gallery. The other key thing was that acknowledged political writers began picking up on ACOSS. It happened because of a deliberate strategy by ACOSS. We focused on putting out press releases that were the reaction of a serious player to major public policy decisions, not just ACOSS condemns etc.".[32]

Disney's role appears to have been crucial. According to Mark Lyons: "Julian was a media natural, good at the short grab, good at longer considered statements and not fazed by it at all. And they respected him for that, particularly the Canberra gallery. And that's really important because ministers and their staff judge what's important by whom the Gallery thinks is important".[33]

By 1996, ACOSS could cite almost 3,000 annual references in press, radio and television.[34] The media's interest in ACOSS in turn arguably reinforced the government's perception of ACOSS as an important and influential lobby group. However, ACOSS still struggled to attain regular coverage in the popular electronic media. This appears to have been because they wanted a "poor person with a crying child rather than ACOSS' views. We don't play those games".[35]

ACOSS acknowledged that weaknesses still existed in its lobbying strategy reflecting the overall political quiescence of the welfare sector. Although thousands of community welfare organizations were involved in service provision, the sector generally failed to organize an effective grass-roots political and electoral movement against poverty.[36] In particular, ACOSS struggled to politically mobilize welfare consumers.

According to the then Victorian Council of Social Service Director and ACOSS Board member Rob Hudson: "It's very hard to organize groups of the unemployed and sole parents to demonstrate. They can't withdraw their labour, and often they feel stigmatized and don't like to make a public fuss about their situation. You're not likely to get 10,000 consumers on the streets and often that's what the government responds to".[37] Similarly former ACOSS President Merle Mitchell noted: "If you're absolutely dependent for your next meal on unemployment benefits you won't risk not getting that cheque. Most rallies are very middle-class. On the whole, most consumers would be too fearful to take public action".[38]

ACOSS' Relationship with the Commonwealth Government

ACOSS developed a much improved relationship with the Labor Party Government. To be sure, the Council continued to be critical of the government's emphasis on low taxation and social expenditure restraint. These criticisms sometimes provoked public displeasure from the government. But at the same time ACOSS balanced its criticisms of government policy by publicly praising those measures with which it was in agreement.

This pragmatic approach helped ACOSS attain unprecedented access to the government. This included regular meetings with the Prime Minister, leading government ministers and public servants. ACOSS was also represented on numerous government forums and advisory bodies pertaining to economics, women, housing, employment, health, social security, taxation, legal aid and family law, and leading government figures including successive Prime Ministers Bob Hawke and Paul Keating regularly spoke at ACOSS' congresses. ACOSS was recognized by government as the legitimate representative of the community welfare sector.[39]

ACOSS projected itself as a key interest group similar to other peak councils such as the Australian Council of Trade Unions and the Business

Council of Australia, albeit whilst acknowledging that it enjoyed less influence.[40] Nevertheless, ACOSS seems to have become an increasingly effective lobby group, and was able to cite numerous policy changes and initiatives which can be attributed wholly or partly to its lobbying activities.

For example, they had significant input into the 1987 Family Assistance Package, which raised assistance to low-income families and substantially reduced the number of children living in poverty.[41] According to former ACOSS Director Mark Lyons, the May 1987 letter from the major church leaders organized by ACOSS was particularly effective. The letter appeared in most Australian papers just before an important cabinet meeting called to discuss the extent to which the Hawke Government would commit itself to a family assistance package and the extent to which they would campaign on it in the federal election, and was arguably "vital in persuading a larger commitment than otherwise would have been given".[42]

Other areas of ACOSS influence appear to have included the increased expenditure on public infrastructure as reflected in the Better Cities Program, expanded child care services, a more flexible income security system, greater recognition of the effectiveness of public housing, increased promotion of trade and industry development, a more equitable system of superannuation tax concessions, the removal of several major loopholes and distortions in the business tax system, the introduction of the Child Support Scheme, the introduction of a national dental health program, increased rent assistance, and the substantial labour market initiatives announced in Working Nation.[43]

ACOSS also failed to influence government on numerous occasions, and had little success in tackling the small government/economic rationalist philosophy that dominated the Labor Government's agenda.[44] For example, ACOSS' campaign for a jobs development levy and other fiscal measures to restore the declining revenue base were rejected. ACOSS appears to have been effective only when its agenda did not fundamentally clash with that of the government.

Funding

ACOSS achieved some success in reducing its dependency on government assistance by increasing the level of self-generated income from sources such as sales of ACOSS publications and project management. By 1996, self-generated revenue represented more than 45 per cent of ACOSS' core budget.[45]

Nevertheless, ACOSS' still significant dependence on its government grant potentially exposed the Council to threats of funding cuts when it was publicly critical of government or opposition policies.[46] ACOSS assured supporters that its "receipt of government funding has not compromised our honest, detailed analysis of the policies of all parties".[47] However, the 1994 Industry Commission Inquiry into Charitable Organizations suggested that peak welfare councils would be more effective if they were financially autonomous – that is, able to advocate or represent their views without fear of reprisal through cuts to funding.[48]

Case Study of Social Action: The Day of Action on Unemployment

During the 1990–92 recession, ACOSS argued vigorously for a more active approach by government to stimulate economic and employment growth.

This campaign included the organization of a Day of Action on Unemployment in May 1992 by a steering committee involving representatives of five major Christian welfare agencies headed by Father John Usher from Centacare. The steering committee appointed contacts in each state, and the State Councils of Social Service were also heavily involved. These state contacts located delegation leaders who were then responsible for establishing delegations. The delegations were drawn from a wide range of local organizations, including church and welfare groups, unions, community workers, and unemployed people. Delegations were provided with an Issues Paper containing background information on unemployment, proposed measures to tackle the problem, and a refutation of likely ALP and Liberal Party responses.[49]

Over 1000 people from 206 local community delegations visited their Federal Members of Parliament to press for action to reduce unemployment including a sustainable increase in jobs, expanded work experience and training programs, and an increased level of income support for unemployed people. More than ninety five per cent of all MPs and senators were visited.[50]

The day of action received wide press and radio coverage, and was reportedly described by *The Australian* as one of the most intense direct lobbying campaigns ever mounted. But there was surprisingly little television coverage given the photo opportunities involved. According to Garth Noweland-Foreman: "We found they had very clear views or stereotypes about what to report on. They saw the unemployed as victims, not as people doing something for themselves. So, they are quite happy to show queues in soup kitchens, but when it came to the unemployed taking action, it was not so interesting because it didn't fit with their preconceptions regarding a story on unemployment".[51]

The Day of Action seems to have had some impact on the national debate on unemployment. One week later the Prime Minister announced that a national summit on youth unemployment would be held in July, and the Liberal Party also organized a summit on unemployment in conjunction with its July national convention.

Questions for Discussion

➤ Discuss the positives and negatives of ACOSS' decision to engage pragmatically with the Labor Government's economic rationalist agenda.

➤ How important was ACOSS' increased media profile in boosting their political influence?

➤ Did ACOSS fail to engage sufficiently with the concerns of unemployed people?

5

Protecting the Welfare Safety Net, 1996–2006

The neo-liberal policies of the Liberal/National Party Coalition Government placed the welfare sector firmly on the defensive. The government actively sought both to reduce the welfare state, and to limit the access and influence of welfare advocacy groups.[1]

As a result, much of ACOSS' energy appears to have been devoted to blocking proposed cutbacks to social programs and spending and to defending its right to participate in public policy debates, rather than to promoting alternative policy or program directions.

ACOSS' capacity to use traditional "insider" lobbying strategies to pressure government seems to have been significantly reduced.[2] Instead, ACOSS turned more to pro-active "outsider" lobbying strategies such as mobilizing public opinion through the media, utilising the influence of its constituency, particularly the longer non-government charities, and developing new and flexible alliances.

Nevertheless, ACOSS maintained its recognized role as "the peak council of the community welfare sector, and the national voice for the needs of people affected by poverty and inequality".[3] ACOSS has continued to expand its representation, and now has almost 70 full member organizations plus 400 associate members. ACOSS describes itself as representing "people at the margins of society. These are the Australians who have an unacceptable standard of living, whether it be because they are unemployed, raising children on low incomes or have health and disability issues. Indigenous disadvantage also covers most of these elements of disadvantage".[4]

Consumers

A number of consumer groups including those representing the disabled, single mothers and Aborigines have attained ongoing positions on the ACOSS Board, and contribute regularly to ACOSS Congresses.

However, the unemployed still lack effective representation. To be sure, ACOSS began to actively assist local unemployed workers' groups in a number of rural and urban areas,[5] and declared that the "voices of unemployed people should be heard by the community, business, unions and government".[6] ACOSS also provided some logistical assistance to the Brisbane-based National Organization for the Unemployed headed by Kevin Brennan and Ron Baker,[7] and some unemployed activists have spoken at ACOSS Congresses. ACOSS could further empower the unemployed by ensuring that they have a representative on the ACOSS Board, and are guaranteed regular input into ACOSS deliberations on unemployment.

ACOSS Objectives and Activities

ACOSS seeks to build "a fair, inclusive and sustainable Australia where all individuals and communities have the resources they need to participate in and benefit from social and economic life".[8]

ACOSS has persistently contested the government's neo-liberal agenda of smaller government, lower taxation and greater private provision of welfare. For example, they argued that the government's initial budget relied too rigidly on expenditure cuts and restraint, rather than the raising of greater public revenue to repair the budget deficit. ACOSS also suggested that concerns about growing poverty and inequality needed to be addressed by more government intervention in the economy rather than via undue reliance on the private sector and free market.

From mid-1996 till the Federal election of August 1998, ACOSS played a central role in Australia's tax reform debate.[9] ACOSS has consistently favoured a more progressive and equitable tax system that would increase the amount of revenue available for support programs for low-income earners. In particular, ACOSS has argued for higher taxes on high-income earners such as taxes on capital gains, fringe benefits, and wealth, the abolition of tax concessions for superannuation payments, the abolition of negative gearing on property investments, and an end to business tax loopholes and distortions. ACOSS has also claimed that Australia is a low taxing country compared to the international average.

ACOSS historically opposed proposals for consumption taxes on the grounds that they were regressive – taking a proportionately larger sum out of a small income than out of a large one. However, from mid-1996, ACOSS suggested in its public statements that it was no longer opposed in principle to a goods and services tax (GST). This reflected ACOSS' increasing concern at the fall in government tax revenue, and its implications for government spending on community services. ACOSS did not favour a new consumption tax or GST in isolation, but supported consideration of an extended Wholesale Sales Tax or National Consumption Tax as part of a broader tax reform package which maintained or improved the progressive nature of the system, and broadened and strengthened the tax base.

ACOSS established an informal alliance with the powerful business sector to promote tax reform. In October 1996, for example, ACOSS and the Australian Chamber of Commerce and Industry (ACCI) revived the dormant tax debate by co-convening the National Tax Reform Summit. The Summit gained nationwide media coverage, and suggested the possibility of welfare and business groups jointly agreeing on a tax package which would meet both equity and efficiency concerns. Subsequently, ACOSS and ACCI formed a Tax Reform Consultative Committee to review proposed reforms, and attempt to attain a consensus.[10] However, in the long-term, the alliance collapsed due to the business sector's perfidy.

Eventually, the Coalition Government adopted a package which conflicted with a number of key ACOSS concerns including opposition to a tax-mix switch, and scepticism about the efficacy of any compensation package. ACOSS was critical of this package, arguing for the exclusion of food from the GST, a reduction in the income tax cuts especially for high income earners, and a serious attempt to close off loopholes and shelters in the personal income tax system.[11] ACOSS subsequently welcomed the exclusion of food from the package, but argued that the package was still unfair due to the regressive tax cuts, and the failure to close loopholes.

ACOSS has continued to defend welfare programs and the rights of welfare recipients. The Council has rejected claims of widespread welfare fraud, arguing that most overpayments are the result of administrative errors or people wrongly estimating their future incomes for the purpose of family payment.[12] ACOSS has also undertaken comparative research showing that government spending on social security, as a proportion of GDP, is well below the OECD average.

ACOSS played a major role in the welfare reform debate, rejecting the government's emphasis on behavioural/individualistic explanations of poverty, and its reliance on key neo-liberal concepts such as welfare dependency and mutual obligation. Instead, ACOSS offered a structural analysis of poverty and inequality, which emphasized the important role played by income support payments in supporting those with no other sources of income, especially where this has occurred through no fault of their own.

ACOSS condemned the government's lop-sided interpretation of mutual obligation, pointing out that Australian unemployment policies had long been based on the joint responsibilities of both the unemployed and government. Governments were obliged to promote full employment, and to reasonably compensate those who were still unable to secure work, whilst the unemployed were obliged to actively seek work, and to accept any reasonable job offers. In contrast, mutual obligation imposed extended obligations on unemployed people without requiring the government to reciprocate by providing access to employment and training opportunities.

ACOSS attacked the introduction of the Work for the Dole scheme, describing it as primarily a welfare compliance program rather than a genuine employment assistance scheme. ACOSS argued that Work for the Dole fails to address the particular skill and experience needs of individual jobseekers, provides poor employment outcomes compared to other labour market programs, and is primarily designed to discipline, punish and control the victims of unemployment.[13]

ACOSS responded with a mixture of praise and caution to the two reports of the Reference Group on Welfare Reform. On the one hand, ACOSS welcomed the Group's focus on encouraging social and economic participation beyond a narrow labour market focus, rationalising the complex payment structure, and improving support services to welfare consumers. However, ACOSS emphasized that the proposals would only promote better outcomes if they reaffirmed the legislated entitlements of the income security safety net, provided for an increase in existing payments above the poverty line as part of a simplified and fairer payment system, and created new and additional resources and opportunities. ACOSS also opposed the extension of mutual obligation requirements to sole parents and the disabled unless extra resources and supports were provided, and if breaching policies were reformed.

ACOSS was very critical of the welfare to work legislation introduced via the 2005 Budget, arguing that the lower incomes for new applicants for sole parent payments and the Disability Support Pension would lower their capacity to meet housing, food, medical and other essential costs. ACOSS urged major amendments pertaining to additional employment assistance, the removal of the anomalies between pension and allowance payments, more assistance with the costs of job search, training and employment, and more substantial government investment in employment and support services.[14]

ACOSS has consistently raised concerns about the growth in long-term unemployment. ACOSS was critical of the introduction of the private Job Network, identifying a number of problems including inadequate funding of providers, limited access to services in rural and regional locations, a poor level and range of services for long-term unemployed people, and generally poor employment outcomes compared to the earlier Working Nation labour programs.[15] ACOSS also contested the official unemployment figure, claiming that over 700,000 "hidden unemployed" people are excluded from the official statistics, and that the real unemployment rate is over 12 per cent compared to the official rate of five per cent.

ACOSS substantially increased its support for the rights and aspirations of indigenous Australians. ACOSS was a foundation member of Australians for Native Title and Reconciliation, actively promoted the justice and recon-ciliation process, issued a formal public "Statement of Apology and Commitment" following the National Inquiry into the forced removal of Aboriginal children from their families, and urged increased expenditure on Aboriginal employment services, housing, health and education.[16] ACOSS also co-opted a senior Indigenous leader to their Board, and in late 2002 established for the first time an ACOSS Indigenous Policy Adviser group. ACOSS strongly opposed the abolition of the Aboriginal and Torres Strait Islander Commission (ATSIC).

ACOSS has vigorously defended the right of publicly-funded welfare advocacy groups and peak bodies to dissent from government policy. In 1998, ACOSS coordinated an open letter from 76 community organizations to all major political parties, calling for a public commitment to "provide public funding for the public voices of those who would otherwise not be heard because they lack power and financial resources".[17]

ACOSS utilized public forums and events such as the 1996 United Nations International Year for the Eradication of Poverty, and the 2004 Senate Inquiry into Poverty and Financial Hardship to express concern about increasing levels of poverty. The final Senate Inquiry into Poverty report emphasized a number of key ACOSS concerns including inadequate employment assistance, the link between low wages and poverty, the increasing demands on emergency relief services, the need for higher income security payments, and a proposed national anti-poverty strategy.[18]

ACOSS also intervened for the first time in national wage cases, priori-tizing wage rises for low paid workers, and arguing that the Industrial Relations Commission should establish an appropriate benchmark for the adequacy of minimum wages. ACOSS opposed junior rates of pay based solely on age, and rejected arguments of a "trade off" between high levels of minimum wages and unemployment.

ACOSS expressed concern about the link between social inequality and poor health. ACOSS argued for maintaining the universal basis of the Medicare system, and opposed the introduction of tax rebates for people with private health insurance. In addition, ACOSS proposed the reinstatement of a dental health scheme for low income earners.

ACOSS also conducted a number of "Living on the Edge" surveys to document rising levels of social distress as reflected in increasing demands on community welfare agencies, argued unsuccessfully for the recognition of advocacy as a legitimate activity in Charities legislation, played a key role in the establishment of the National Roundtable of Non-profit organizations, and argued for improved access to affordable and secure housing via greater investment in public and community housing, and improved rent assistance.

ACOSS condemned the racism associated with Pauline Hanson's One Nation movement, opposed the war in Iraq, questioned the introduction of contracting and compulsory competitive tendering for human services funding, urged the development of more affordable and high quality child care services, condemned mandatory sentencing in the Northern Territory, published three annual reports on National emergency relief data, hosted a seminar on community capacity building within government and the community sector, and undertook a major research project on philanthropy in Australia.

Other ACOSS priorities included addressing the particular disadvantages experienced by low income people in rural and regional Australia, adequate funding of legal aid services, liaising with the welfare sector both to develop their capacity to influence public policy and to gain from their policy expertise and knowledge, maintaining equitable access to residential aged care facilities, advocating alternatives to mandatory detention for refugees and asylum seekers, opposing the increased cost of higher education, and rejecting proposals for shared custody of children on separation.

ACOSS has also begun to engage with the debate around economic globalization, and the potential detrimental impact of global financial pressures on national levels of poverty and inequality. ACOSS acknowledge that governments are using the rhetoric of globalization as an excuse to justify the introduction of free market policies. But they explicitly reject the argument that financial markets have undermined the power of national governments to set their own social and economic agendas. Rather they claim that the Australian Government is still in control of its spending and taxation options, and that non-government organizations retain the capacity to influence government decisions.[19]

ACOSS' International Policy Committee has critically examined the impact of powerful international trading and investment bodies and treaties such as the World Trade Organization and the deferred Multilateral

Agreement on Investment on human rights and social justice in Australia. ACOSS has drawn attention to the absence of democratic structures in such bodies, and to their promotion of unfair trade rules and regulations.[20] ACOSS has consistently argued for the development of new international institutions to establish binding social, labour and environmental standards that duplicate national controls in these areas, and match existing universal regulations on human rights, health promotion, transportation safety, postal and telephonic services etc.

ACOSS has recognized the need to expand its regional and international links as a means of promoting a strengthened global civil society distinct from both government and the free market.[21] The Council has been a significant participant in the Asia-Pacific Region of the International Council on Social Welfare (ICSW) with former ACOSS leader Michael Raper active as the current President, and provided modest support to ACOSS representative Julian Disney during his time as World President of the ICSW from 1996–2000. ACOSS has also held regular meetings with governments and non-government organizations (NGOs) in South East Asia, and is engaged with regional civil society projects. For example, ACOSS was contracted by the Asian Development Bank to promote the active involvement of NGOs and other civil society groups in Papua New Guinea and Fiji in government budget decision-making processes and policy development.[22]

However, these regional and international activities and alliances are still limited in their application. For example, ACOSS opposed the Australia-US Free Trade Agreement because they were concerned that it could have an adverse impact on the Pharmaceutical Benefits Scheme which guarantees affordable medicine to most Australians. But ACOSS does not appear to have identified any common concerns or formed any links with US health or welfare NGOs during this campaign. And most of ACOSS' international activities (with the possible exception of the Free Trade Agreement campaign) seem to have been undertaken in relative isolation from their other activities on behalf of Australian low income earners.

Ideology

ACOSS continued to espouse a social democratic ideology based on "tackling the causes of inequality and disadvantage rather than just the symptoms".[23] ACOSS drew attention to evidence of increasing social divisions, and emphasized not only the increasing number of people living in poverty, but also the emergence of a powerful and unaccountable "overclass" of high income earners.[24]

But in practice, much of ACOSS' advocacy work involved responding to incremental changes in government welfare policy, rather than promoting a broader structural reform agenda. This contradiction frustrated ACOSS President Andrew McCallum who argued the importance of "making ourselves central to debates that enhance the lives of all Australians and not be content to pick up the pieces or relegated to the margins when social policy debates of substance take place".[25]

Ideological Critics

A number of left-wing critics attacked ACOSS' willingness to consider changes to the indirect taxation system including a goods and services tax. They argued instead that a progressive tax on the rich and on company profits was the only equitable basis of a taxation system.[26] However, no serious strategies were proposed as to how such ideas might be effectively introduced into the mainstream political debate.

Neo-liberal commentators have continued to criticize the activities of ACOSS and the welfare lobby, calling them unelected and unrepresentative, and suggesting that their main concern is their own professional advancement, rather than the relief of poverty. For example, former National Party Senator John Stone attacked ACOSS during the tax reform debate, arguing that it had reversed its opposition to a GST solely because it realized that a new tax was the only means of funding its "ever-growing wish-lists of more, and bigger, social welfare benefits". According to Stone, ACOSS had "by its incessant past spending demands, done more to jeopardize the budgetary outlook than almost any other institution in the country".[27]

Similarly, Institute of Public Affairs Senior Fellow Gary Johns suggested that ACOSS represents its own vested interests and narrow ideological agendas, rather than the poor.[28] He accused ACOSS and other welfare lobby groups of receiving more than $3 million of government funding per year under false pretences. Johns claimed that information about ACOSS' real activities was denied to the public.[29]

The Centre for Independent Studies has repeatedly attacked ACOSS, claiming that they deliberately exaggerate levels of poverty, object to any attempts to promote greater self-reliance amongst welfare recipients, and are primarily motivated by a politics of envy.[30] Other neo-liberal critics of ACOSS include journalists Paddy McGuiness, Frank Devine and Bettina Arndt. Most of these criticisms appear to be driven by ideological prejudice, rather than by any serious analysis of the welfare state or welfare advocacy groups.

Lobbying Strategies

ACOSS has utilized a range of strategies to influence the public policy agenda including developing policy based on "independent research and analysis, real experiences and advice from the ACOSS network, the community and other sectors", advocating ACOSS policies to key decision makers, and providing the non-government welfare sector with "information and policy and advocacy leadership on key social, economic and environmental issues".[31]

ACOSS has sought to mobilize its core constituency on key campaigns. For example, ACOSS responded to the establishment of the Reference Group on Welfare Reform by organizing 20 community forums around the country to consult with the community welfare sector, and fuel their energy. ACOSS also sought to form alliances with other peak bodies around specific issues of mutual concern such as child care, housing, employment services, and disability, and contributed to the formation of a National Coalition Against Poverty.[32]

Similarly, ACOSS utilized a number of strategies to influence the Welfare to Work debate including a new online action network campaign directed at local members of parliament, and an Advocacy Day in Canberra. The Advocacy Day involved over 60 welfare activists participating in meetings with Ministers and Shadow Ministers and a further 40 parliamentarians.[33]

ACOSS has also formed a range of political alliances including the ill-fated partnership with the business sector to promote tax reform,[34] and the Services First group formed to persuade government to give priority to investment in health and community services rather than to tax cuts. Other coalitions have included the Friends of Medicare alliance, the Healthcare Reform alliance, the National Affordable Housing alliance, the Community Care Coalition, the Disability Participation alliance, and the Dental Health alliance.

In addition, ACOSS has participated in the Australian Collaboration project alongside a number of conservation, ethnic, Aboriginal, church and other community groups. The project aims at promoting a socially, culturally and environmentally sustainable Australia, and has produced two major reports titled "A Just and Sustainable Australia" and "Where are we going: comprehensive social, cultural, environmental and economic reporting".

ACOSS has also worked closely with minor parties in the Senate to influence policy outcomes. For example, ACOSS appear to have advised the Democrats during the tax reform debate,[35] and later on the 2003 Australians Working Together Bill.[36] More recently, ACOSS has collaborated with the

Australian Greens to raise concerns about the government's welfare to work legislation.[37]

ACOSS' Relationship with the Commonwealth Government

ACOSS' relationship with the current Liberal-National Coalition Government has been less than harmonious. In part, this tension has reflected the deep ideological gulf between ACOSS and the Coalition. The government favours a neo-liberal agenda, whereas ACOSS remains wedded to a traditional social democratic approach.

Hence, ACOSS has been regularly critical of government policies. For example, ACOSS vigorously contested the 1996 federal budget, rejecting the large cuts to labour market programs, Aboriginal assistance and legal aid, the abolition of the dental health program, and cuts to other welfare payments and programs which disproportionately hit low income households.[38] ACOSS has also strongly opposed other government policies including the work for the dole scheme, cuts to public housing, the private health insurance and savings rebate, and the two year social security waiting period for migrants.

In addition, ACOSS argued for significant modifications to the Common Youth Allowance scheme and private Job Network. At the same time, ACOSS praised policies with which it was in agreement such as the Stronger Families and Communities Strategy, the maintenance of pension rates at 25 per cent of average earnings, additional payments to carers, the new working credits scheme, and increases to the Family Tax Benefit.

Equally, the government has, under the influence of public choice theory, actively sought at times to exclude and marginalize ACOSS. This strategy was first reflected in the government's blackballing of ACOSS during the final stages of the GST tax debate due to ACOSS' opposition to the government's final policy proposal. Most notably, the government chose not to appoint any ACOSS representative to the Reference Group on Welfare Reform despite ACOSS' key role in the welfare policy debate. Nor was ACOSS granted a representative on the Welfare Reform Consultative Forum. And leading Ministers such as Peter Costello and Tony Abbott were at times brutally critical of ACOSS.[39]

However, ACOSS still retains a significant degree of access to government.[40] The Prime Minister John Howard has consistently emphasized his commitment to dialogue with ACOSS despite differences of opinion.[41] During 2004–2005, for example, ACOSS held formal meetings with the

Prime Minister, Treasurer, and two other senior Ministers, plus numerous meetings with leading Commonwealth bureaucrats. Leading government figures also spoke regularly at ACOSS Congresses, and ACOSS was represented on numerous government advisory groups. It would appear that the government sees regular contact with ACOSS as a means of pacifying, or at least negotiating with, a potentially critical, or even damaging, interest group.

But direct negotiations with and appeals to government have had only limited impact on policy outcomes. Most ACOSS proposals and criticisms of government policy have been rejected by the government. ACOSS has had to identify new and more effective means to influence government policy. ACOSS has still claimed some victories including the Coalition's initial commitment to maintaining existing rates and benchmarks for income security payments, although ACOSS later acknowledged that this commitment had only been honoured by a "selective and narrow definition" of the welfare safety net.[42]

On welfare reform, ACOSS successfully mobilized the views and concerns of its large and varied community welfare constituency. It appears that ACOSS advocacy played a significant role in shifting the welfare reform debate from its original punitive emphasis on addressing alleged welfare dependency to a more positive agenda of promoting greater opportunities and participation.[43] ACOSS also enjoyed some initial success in assisting disability groups to defeat the proposed tightening of the Disability Support Pension announced in the 2002 federal Budget.[44] And ACOSS managed to influence some improvements to the 2005 Welfare to Work Bill including retaining Parenting Payment for single parents until their youngest child turns eight instead of six, and exemptions from activity requirements for a number of recipient groups.[45]

In addition, ACOSS claims that its intervention in the tax debate produced a far better outcome than would otherwise have occurred. For example, ACOSS appears to have won a number of concessions from its dialogue with the government and the minor parties including the squashing of early government proposals to reduce overall tax revenue, and to directly use the GST to fund big personal income tax cuts, the removal of basic food from the GST, an improved compensation package, and the addressing of poverty traps caused by the interaction of the tax and social security systems.[46]

But most of these examples seem to have involved the defence of existing programs and policies, rather than the promotion of alternative directions. ACOSS also seems to have spent considerable time and energy defending its right to participate in public policy debates. As a result it appears that both its political expectations and relative effectiveness have declined.[47]

Funding

ACOSS continues to be dependent on its annual government grant for about 42 per cent of its funding, but this is a significant reduction from the early 1990s figure of 59 per cent. Other major contributions to ACOSS' current income of approximately $1,180,000 come from membership fees and donations (26 per cent), annual congress income (12 per cent), publications income (7 per cent), project management (6 per cent), and fees for services (4 per cent).

ACOSS recognizes the danger of this limited funding base for its political independence, and is seeking to diversify and broaden its sources of income, to increase the level of long-term support from philanthropic donors and corporate sponsors, and to increase its financial reserves.[48]

Case Study of Social Action: Social Security Breaches [49]

One consequence of the government's mutual obligation policies was the introduction of tougher requirements on the unemployed, including the expectation that they seek up to ten jobs each fortnight. Recipients who failed to meet these obligations were increasingly subjected to social security breaches, and associated heavy fines.

Overall, there was an increase in the number of breaches from 120,000 in 1997–98 to 386,000 in 2000–2001 – an increase of 187% in three years. This included a significant rise in both the percentage of unemployed allowance recipients incurring breach penalties, and the number of individuals incurring multiple breach penalties.[50] These breaches caused increased demand from low income people for emergency relief and financial aid services, and placed considerable pressure on charities and community welfare agencies.

In conjunction with the National Welfare Rights Network, ACOSS expressed significant concerns about breaching practices including the increasing numbers of unemployed people being breached, the disproportionate financial penalties imposed which compared harshly to the average fines for serious criminal offences, the considerable financial hardship experienced by those breached, and the high number of particularly disadvantaged jobseekers being breached including young people, Indigenous Australians and those with social and mental health deficits.

ACOSS utilized a number of strategies to progress its concerns including formal written submissions, media releases, and alliances. ACOSS' written submissions tended to be particularly persuasive. They typically included well-researched empirical data on the extent of breaches, emphasized that breaches were incurred for often unintentional infringements of complex rules rather than for fraud, and presented detailed case studies which demonstrated the particular difficulties faced by disadvantaged groups.[51]

In addition, ACOSS organized a joint statement by national peak community and consumer organizations, charities and church welfare agencies including a number of specialist agencies dealing with particularly vulnerable groups such as Aborigines, the homeless, the drug & alcohol dependent, and those with acquired brain injury. Released in December 2000, the statement called on the government to overhaul the existing system of social security penalties – both the rules and the penalties.[52]

ACOSS also co-sponsored an independent review of social security breaches and penalties with a number of non-government welfare organizations such as Mission Australia, the Salvation Army, Jobs Australia, Job Futures Limited, and the Smith Family. Whilst these organizations are all members of ACOSS, they are also major Job Network providers, and known for their good relations with the Howard Government. Their involvement helped to deter any questions about the independence or integrity of the review process. The Pearce Review, as it became known, made 36 detailed recommendations aimed at promoting a fairer and more effective system.[53]

Later, ACOSS formed a Breaching and Penalties Taskforce consisting of the group of non-government welfare and community organizations which had co-sponsored the Pearce Review, in order to promote support for the Pearce Review recommendations. ACOSS also sent out Briefing and Action notes to all their supporters in November 2002 urging member organizations and their affiliates as well as community members to support the call for reduction to the duration and rate of breach penalties through amendments to the Australians Working Together Bill. Recipients of the notes were asked to participate in a letter writing campaign, to distribute the material to others in the community, to write to relevant Ministers and Opposition Senators, and to create news and publicity about the negative consequences of the existing breaching policy.[54]

ACOSS appears to have enjoyed significant success on the breaching issue. For example, many of the recommendations of the Pearce Review were specifically endorsed by the Senate Community Affairs Committee Inquiry into the Australians Working Together Bill.[55] In addition, the Commonwealth Ombudsman's Report confirmed the findings of the earlier ACOSS reports, and the Pearce Review.

The recommendations of the Pearce Review and associated Senate and

Ombudsman's inquiries produced significant changes in government policy and practice.[56] There appears to have been a major improvement in Centrelink breaching processes, and there is evidence that the total number of breaches has fallen. For example, the number of breaches in the year 2002–3 was only 130,000, less than one-third of the earlier peak figure.[57]

ACOSS' lobbying also appears to have been influential in the Senate debate on the Australians Working Together Bill. After the Senate blocked the initial Bill, the government subsequently agreed to the Democrat's amendments in March 2003 – strongly supported by ACOSS – which softened breaching penalties for one-off offences.[58] This meant that the majority of unemployed people breached for the first time had their breach period reduced from 26 weeks (or 13 weeks for an administrative breach) to eight weeks. The associated penalty went down from $890 to $270. In addition, ACOSS was allocated two representatives on the new Taskforce which has been formed to review the breaching system. Nevertheless, no changes have been made to penalties for second and third breaches.

Questions for Discussion

➤ Discuss the merits and limitations of ACOSS' high profile intervention in the taxation debate.

➤ Are there other potentially more effective strategies that ACOSS could have undertaken to respond to the political and ideological challenge posed by globalisation?

➤ Has ACOSS given sufficient priority to the needs and concerns of indigenous Australians?

6

Labourists and Welfarists

The relationship between the Federal Labor Party and the Australian Council of Social Service

The Australian Council of Social Service and the Federal Australian Labor Party (ALP) have often been depicted as political allies due to the relative symmetry of their ideological positions. However, the historical record suggests that their relationship is far more complex than an alliance would suggest. To be sure, ACOSS has arguably enjoyed greater access and influence during periods of ALP rule. But equally, many of ACOSS' most serious conflicts have occurred with ALP governments.

It would seem that this mixture of cooperation and conflict reflects the differing organizational concerns and priorities of political parties and interest groups. The ALP is concerned to lock in political support from groups on the non-conservative side of the spectrum, and seems to regard ACOSS as a type of additional party faction which is expected to offer unconditional public loyalty in return for having some of its policy agenda adopted.

In contrast, ACOSS' priority is the implementation of policies designed to benefit its low income constituency (many of which coincide with the ALP platform), irrespective of the political compromises faced by labour parties seeking to win and maintain power. ACOSS appears to have greater expectations of, and makes greater demands on, the ALP than Liberal-National Coalition governments, but is not willing to trade away its party-political independence in return.

Interest Groups and Policy Making

A number of theoretical approaches have been used to analyze the role of interest groups in society including pluralism, corporatism, public choice theory, and Marxism.[1] In contrast to these grand theories or frameworks, Smith's notion of policy networks arguably better explains the real nature of relationships between governments and interest groups.

According to this notion, the state is not a unified body with a single set of interests. Rather, it includes a range of departments, sections within departments, agencies and actors who have different interests. These varied state actors may in turn elect to adopt particular policies, or consult particular interest groups. Policy networks or communities exist when there is some exchange of resources between the state and interest groups. This can range from a limited exchange of information to the institutionalization of an approved group in the policy process.[2]

Sawer and Jupp expand on this analysis by documenting the particular interactions between state actors and the peak bodies representing women, consumers, health issues, AIDS, and the environment. They argue that these relationships are a "two-way street", and that state actors often utilise peak bodies to influence policy agendas. The nature of this relationship will be influenced by the professionalization and institutionalization of the peak bodies including their organizational strength, and the electoral and political standing of their constituency.[3] As we shall see, ACOSS provides a strong example of policy institutionalization not only through its formal incorporation into government decision-making processes, but also via its membership of the ALP's own social policy network.

ACOSS and the ALP, 1956–1975

In its early years, ACOSS was largely controlled by a combination of religious welfare agencies, other conservative charities, and professional doctors and social workers.[4] The organization seems to have had only limited contact with the ALP, although some lobbying of ALP parliamentarians was undertaken during the 1962 campaign for civilian widows with dependent children.[5]

This lack of contact reflected both pragmatic and ideological influences. ACOSS' principal priority was to establish friendly relations with the dominant Liberal-National Coalition Government, and to secure if possible both government recognition and financial assistance. In contrast, the ALP seemed politically insignificant, and to sections of the ACOSS leadership, dangerously radical.

For example, the Victorian branch of the Australian Association of Social Workers, a major affiliate of ACOSS and by no means their most conservative member, refused a 1965 request from the Victorian ALP to provide expert information on social welfare matters due to a concern about being associated with the ALP's socialist political philosophy.[6] The AASW also appears to have discouraged links between social workers and the trade union movement.[7]

In the late 1960s and early 1970s, ACOSS became more critical of government policies particularly around health insurance and social security payments. There is some evidence that ACOSS established links with the ALP around these issues. For example, ALP leader Gough Whitlam was a guest speaker at the 1970 ACOSS National Conference, and leaders of the ALP began to utilize ACOSS concerns in their policy statements.[8] However, these links provoked tensions within ACOSS with some more conservative elements led by the Australian Medical Association condemning ACOSS's association with the ALP's views on health insurance.[9]

ACOSS welcomed the election of the Whitlam ALP government in December 1972, and generally supported government initiatives. The ACOSS President Judith Green noted positively that "policies which ACOSS and its members have been recommending for many years are one after another being implemented and this must be a cause of satisfaction to all those who care for the disadvantaged in our affluent community".[10] Similarly, the ACOSS submission to the Poverty Inquiry commended the government for taking serious steps "to improve the position of the poor".[11] Overall there was considerable ideological congruence between the government's social democratic viewpoint, and ACOSS' increasing support for universalistic welfare payments.

Nevertheless, some conflict occurred. In part, this reflected inevitable tensions between government bureaucrats and the non-government welfare sector, and particularly ACOSS' unsuccessful expectation that the voluntary sector be directly consulted in the development of government welfare policies. More serious disagreement occurred around ACOSS' reluctance to support the government without qualification. Whilst ACOSS endorsed the government's general direction, it continued to urge that more be done to enhance the opportunities of low income earners. In addition, ACOSS retained ongoing links and discussions with the Liberal Party, and particularly their Shadow Social Security Minister, Don Chipp.

There is evidence that the government, and particularly the Social Security Minister Bill Hayden, became increasingly frustrated with what they considered to be ACOSS' "all or nothing" approach.[12] For example, Hayden would later refer disparagingly to what he called the welfare industry's "extravagant demands" for more spending on welfare services and programs.[13]

Similarly, Hayden's successor, Senator John Wheeldon complained that ACOSS was unwilling to engage with economic and budgetary realities. According to Wheeldon, "I well remember that when shortly before the presentation of the 1975 Budget, I made a speech to an ACOSS conference in which I argued that the predicted Budget deficit was so unacceptably high that we had to delay the introduction of some of the welfare programs that we had intended to follow, the response of ACOSS was both uncomprehending and hostile". Wheeldon added that he felt "ACOSS was unduly confrontational towards a Labor government, which, it should have recognized, was much more sympathetic towards its general objectives than were the Opposition parties".[14]

Tensions came to a head following the 1975 federal budget. ACOSS had earlier requested a total annual funding package of approximately $470,000 which included a core grant of $156,000 for ACOSS (up from $115,000 in 1974–75), and over $300,000 (up from $60,000 in 1974–75) for the activities of the eight State and Territory Councils of Social Service. ACOSS believed this proposal had been endorsed by the then Minister, Bill Hayden. However, the new Minister, Senator John Wheeldon, reduced ACOSS' core grant to $90,000, and provided no funding for the state affiliates.

Various theories were offered as to the reasons for the funding cut. On the one hand, the 1975 Budget was designed to reduce inflation and the budget deficit, and many community groups experienced cuts in government funding. It has also been suggested by Marie Coleman (the former head of the Social Welfare Commission) that ACOSS "failed to come to terms with the difference between a core grant and a project grant, and wrongly assumed that ongoing funding was going to combine the two".[15]

Wheeldon himself explained that the government was faced with a choice between funding policy advocacy and research, or alternatively funding direct services to welfare clients. Given this dilemma, he argued that the government had no choice but to prioritize "paying for rooms and beds for people to sleep in".[16] Wheeldon added that he would prefer to fund an "amenities room for blind workers in Adelaide", rather than funding ACOSS officials to attend international social welfare conferences.[17]

On the other hand, rumours persisted that the government had specifically targeted ACOSS' funding as punishment for various misdemeanours. One story suggested that ACOSS had been penalized for making public criticisms of government policy. Another story referred specifically to the participation of the ACOSS Secretary-General in the Liberal Party's social welfare committee.[18] John Wheeldon later confirmed that he was "not impressed by the apparently close association between at least one prominent member of ACOSS and Don Chipp, the Opposition's Shadow Minister for Health".[19]

ACOSS responded to the funding cut with a large public campaign urging reinstatement of the original funding proposal. A campaign brochure was printed and circulated throughout the welfare sector, and to all members of parliament. The brochure documented ACOSS' activities and achievements, criticized the lack of explanation for the funding cuts, and defended ACOSS's right and obligation to provide expert advice to people with different political views and affiliation.[20] ACOSS' campaign was supported by leading members of the Liberal Party opposition including Party leader Malcolm Fraser, and Senator Peter Baume.[21]

The campaign had some impact on the ALP government. Senator Wheeldon acknowledged that the funding cut may have been too severe, and added sarcastically, "If I may strike a historical note, Mr Chairman, you may remember that before Queen Mary I passed on, she said that after she died they would find two names engraved on her heart, Philip and Calais. I am afraid that two names could be well engraved on my heart, if I were to pass on shortly, and they would be ACOSS and International Social Services".[22] Following negotiations with both Wheeldon and Treasurer Hayden, the government announced an additional grant of $60,000 to ACOSS in October 1975.[23]

ACOSS and the ALP, 1975–1983

After the dismissal of the Whitlam Government, ACOSS resumed cooperative relations with the federal ALP. ACOSS met regularly with Shadow ALP Ministers (particularly social security spokesperson, Senator Don Grimes) and their staff, and with Labor's Health and Welfare Committee. Senator Grimes also addressed a number of ACOSS conferences. In addition, a number of ACOSS activists were involved in ALP state welfare committees.[24]

Grimes enjoyed strong personal relations with key ACOSS policy officers, Philippa Smith and Joan McLintock. He recalls that "ACOSS looked at legislation fairly carefully. In my view, they gave credit where credit was due either to the government or the opposition. ACOSS was set up as a representative body of all sorts of welfare bodies, and in that period they were very conscious of that. They were representative".[25] Overall the

ALP provided some support for ACOSS' structuralist views,[26] and this support helped ACOSS in its attempts to alter or change government policies.

ACOSS and the ALP, 1983–1996

During the Hawke/Keating years, ACOSS appears to have reached the peak of its influence. The Prime Minister Paul Keating referred to ACOSS as one of a number of "special interest groups representing ordinary Australians" whom the government "deals with, accords status to, learns from, and acts in partnership with",[27] and the Deputy Prime Minister Brian Howe described the government and ACOSS as sharing a "common goal to improve social justice in Australia".[28] In short, ACOSS became an accepted member of the government's "policy network" which meant opportunities to influence and alter government agendas.[29]

The above analysis might suggest a firm political alliance between ACOSS and the ALP government based on common ideological assumptions. However, the actual relationship was far more complex. At times, there was significant and harmonious policy cooperation between the two groups. But equally at other times, there was considerable public conflict. One source of tension existed around the differing interests of paid workers, and those on low incomes. The government favored tax cuts for all workers even those who were higher paid, whilst ACOSS believed that social spending on the poor should be a higher priority. Another source of disagreement was over superannuation.

More generally, confrontation occurred due to differing organizational expectations and priorities. ACOSS expected the ALP government to adhere to its social justice rhetoric, and implement redistributionist policies which favored low income people. When this didn't occur, ACOSS felt no inhibition in criticizing government policies. The ALP, in contrast, believed that presumed allies such as ACOSS should display public loyalty to a government which was at least attempting to promote social justice outcomes. When ACOSS nevertheless broke ranks, the government tended to respond by vigorously questioning its credibility and legitimacy.

According to former ACOSS Deputy President Chris Sidoti, "The ALP expected ACOSS would be head over heels in adulation of them after they were elected because there were traditionally close personal and policy links between ACOSS and the ALP. There was also a somewhat worrisome view in the ALP of itself as so broadly-based that it is capable of containing within ALP debates a whole range of progressive views and opinions so that issues are fought out inside the ALP, not outside. ACOSS was seen as being part of this enormous ALP umbrella, and shouldn't be indulging in public criticism".[30]

The ACOSS–ALP relationship also enjoyed particular peaks and troughs. ACOSS initially developed a fairly harmonious relationship with the Hawke Government which it expected to promote social justice agendas. However, as 1983–84 progressed, ACOSS became more critical of the government.

ACOSS accused the government of "failing to adequately address the expectations that it fostered on Australia's poor". According to ACOSS: "Taxation cuts for political rather than redistributive purposes; almost insignificant increases in pensions and benefits because of rigorous control to contain the deficit; increasingly complex participation mechanisms that disenfranchise those with few resources – all appear to indicate a conscious policy of collusion against the have-nots".[31]

In addition, there was some resentment at the exclusive access granted by the government to the Australian Council of Trade Unions, and an expectation that the government establish a Social Accord with ACOSS to mirror the government's Accord with the ACTU.[32] The ACOSS President Bruce McKenzie emphasized in a letter to Prime Minister Hawke that "the tens of thousands of community and welfare groups do not accept that the ACTU can speak on behalf of the disadvantaged, the unemployed, and pensioners. Nor do we accept the appropriateness of the ACTU alone having special access to discuss tax cuts and welfare expenditure, particularly when expertise in the latter rests overwhelmingly in our sector".[33]

The period of 1984–85 was a low point during which ACOSS became particularly disenchanted with the government's economic rationalist model. ACOSS unsuccessfully employed campaign strategies and public criticism in an attempt to persuade the government to implement ACOSS objectives.

The government responded with furious criticism of ACOSS. Prime Minister Hawke accused ACOSS of economic incompetence for failing to acknowledge the government's success in creating employment. Hawke also criticized ACOSS' bid for increased government funding including an increase in salary for their Secretary-General. Hawke questioned whether ACOSS "may not have a mote in their own eye".[34] The Treasurer Paul Keating also attacked ACOSS, describing them as "economic simpletons", and questioning whether they really represented low income earners.[35] Similarly, Social Security Minister Don Grimes complained that ACOSS had abandoned their role of "being a watchdog of the income security system", and instead focused obsessively on taxation and wealth distribution. According to Grimes: "Some of their proposals were not only impractical and difficult to implement, but you couldn't even understand them".[36]

These attacks seemed to represent a deliberate attempt by the government to intimidate ACOSS into silence, and to reinforce the ALP's contention that allies such as ACOSS should limit their dissent to internal ALP forums. In part, the particular vehemence of this episode appears to have also reflected the poor personal relations between the government, and the then ACOSS leadership team of Director Colin Menzies, and President Bruce McKenzie. Both ALP and ACOSS representatives (e.g. Don Grimes and former ACOSS Deputy President Chris Sidoti) agree that the government was infuriated by Menzies' criticism of government economic policies.[37]

In late 1985, ACOSS elected a new pragmatic leadership consisting of Welfare Rights Centre Coordinator Julian Disney as President and Mark Lyons as Director.[38] From that point onwards, ACOSS continued to criticize government policies, but also attempted to engage and challenge the government from within its defined economic rationalist parameters. ACOSS also gave qualified praise to ALP policies during a number of federal election campaigns, although it was careful not to offer any formal party-political endorsement.[39]

As a result, relations between ACOSS and the government underwent significant improvement, and ACOSS was able to influence a number of government policies. Nevertheless, some tensions continued. Whilst ACOSS President (and later economics spokesperson) Julian Disney enjoyed good relations with Prime Minister Hawke,[40] he was subsequently criticized by Prime Minister Keating who refused on one occasion to see an ACOSS delegation because it included Disney. After some negotiations, however, Keating relented and agreed to see the delegation.[41] Similarly, Keating responded to ACOSS criticisms of proposed tax cuts by arguing that the ACTU rather than ACOSS was the primary representative of low income earners.[42] Keating also gave little time to subsequent ACOSS President Robert Fitzgerald.[43]

ACOSS and the ALP, 1996–2006

Since the election of the Howard Liberal-National Coalition Government, the relationship between the ALP and ACOSS has continued to be characterized by a mixture of cooperation and conflict.

On issues of social security and welfare reform, ACOSS has sought and generally gained support from the ALP in its campaigns against the economic rationalist policies of the Howard Government. For example, the ALP has supported ACOSS' concerns around health services, housing provision, welfare reform, and increased poverty and inequality.[44] The ALP provided strong support for ACOSS' campaign against the Howard Government's harsh breaching policies.[45]

However, on the question of taxation and specifically the government's goods and services tax, ACOSS and the ALP had a major falling out. The ALP was highly critical of ACOSS' willingness to consider a GST, arguing that ACOSS had lent legitimacy to Howard's regressive tax agenda. There was also a perception (rightly or wrongly) that the ACOSS President Robert Fitzgerald was personally and politically close to Prime Minister Howard.[46]

At an acrimonious meeting between Labor MPs and ACOSS representatives, Alison McLelland and Peter Davidson at Parliament House in September 1997, the Labor Senator Stephen Conroy denounced ACOSS, saying: "I have just been sitting here listening to you for the last 20 minutes and I cannot believe what I have just heard". Conroy accused ACOSS of "playing footsies" with the government. In response, Alison McLelland refused to give ground, arguing that ACOSS would support a tax package including a GST providing it was equitable and addressed long-term revenue requirements.[47]

Senior ALP figures including Treasury Spokesperson Gareth Evans subsequently threatened on a number of occasions that ACOSS could face retribution from a future ALP government should it continue to cooperate with the Liberals on tax reform.[48] Matters came to a head during the August 1998 federal election campaign when the ALP released its own tax package based on an unequivocal opposition to a GST, and the tackling of tax loopholes for the affluent.

The ALP's position appeared to be far closer to ACOSS' agenda than that of the government's tax plan which ACOSS had earlier described as "unbalanced and unfair". However, ACOSS was also openly critical of the Labor Party's package, insisting that it failed to strengthen the tax system in relation to income, consumption, and state revenues. For ACOSS, the package was "fair enough, but not good enough".[49] ACOSS' criticism angered the ALP given that it had the potential to adversely impact on the party's election prospects. And it is arguable that ACOSS' political strategy on tax served to benefit the Howard government more than the ALP given that the former was primarily concerned to neutralize potential ACOSS opposition to a GST.[50]

However, ACOSS was never going to simply bow to ALP pressure to moderate its critique of ALP tax policy. ACOSS' broad (and ideologically fluid) constituency expected the Council to maintain its party political independence, and to judge the policies of both parties on their merits. In addition, ACOSS retained some justified skepticism as to the ALP's intentions on tax since it was the previous Labor Government which had permitted the revenue base to decline by such a significant proportion.[51]

The tax debate seemingly continues to leave a shadow over ACOSS/ALP relations. Some leading ALP figures do not appear to have forgiven ACOSS for its flirtation with the Howard Government's GST.[52] For example, leading ALP frontbencher Lindsay Tanner denounced ACOSS for allegedly defending the Howard Government at the expense of ordinary people. Tanner made reference once again to ACOSS' position on the GST.[53]

The former ALP leader Mark Latham was also a regular critic of ACOSS.[54] The tensions between ACOSS and Latham became public during the 2004 federal election campaign when ACOSS criticized the ALP's tax and family package as having a potentially regressive impact on jobless families with two or more children. According to ACOSS, 185,000 families with 500,000 children would be worse off under Labor's proposals.

Mark Latham responded by suggesting that ACOSS wanted to keep people on welfare: "I have a different approach in saying that the best life is not a life of welfare, it's a life of work". According to Latham, what mattered was not "the size of the welfare payment", but rather "the size of the pay packet".[55] Later in his much-publicized *Diaries*, Latham denounced ACOSS as a "Left conservative" body always "whingeing about all the things they don't like in the world. But not offering any answers, other than increased transfer payments".[56]

Conclusion

The relationship between ACOSS and the federal ALP has experienced many twists and turns since the two groups first established regular contact in the late 1960s. Whilst many media and academic commentators have described the groups as traditional political allies, this term tends to oversimplify both the actual historical nature of the relationship, and particularly ACOSS' bipartisan approach to engagement with both major political parties.

To be sure, there has often been close relations between some ACOSS operatives and the ALP, and strong links between ACOSS and the ALP's broad political network. These connections reflect the general symmetry between the ideological perspectives of ACOSS and the ALP. However, unlike the ACTU, ACOSS has never been formally represented within ALP internal debates and processes, nor has ACOSS sought such representation.

Consequently, relations between ACOSS and the ALP have always involved a mixture of cooperation and conflict. This is because the groupings have different agendas. The ALP is concerned to win elections, and to secure the support of interest groups to facilitate such outcomes. It does seek in principle to promote social justice, but this endeavour is arguably secondary to the primary aim of securing power. In contrast, ACOSS seeks to represent its affiliate members, and to promote fairer outcomes for low income people. These outcomes may on balance be better served by the election of ALP rather than Liberal-National Coalition governments, but ACOSS values its political autonomy, and consequently its right to judge specific government policies on their merits free of fear or favor.

Questions for Discussion

➤ Discuss the reasons why ACOSS is often described as an ally of the Australian Labor Party.

➤ Consider the factors which lead to conflict as well as cooperation between ACOSS and the Labor Party.

➤ Why is ACOSS so concerned to retain its political bipartisanship?

7

Neo-liberalism versus Social Justice

The relationship between the Federal Liberal Party and the Australian Council of Social Service

The Australian Council of Social Service and the Federal Liberal Party have often been viewed as political enemies due to their public clashes over taxation and social expenditure. Yet the historical record suggests that this description may be an exaggeration particularly when applied to the earlier years of ACOSS activity. For much of this period ACOSS' relationship with the Liberals was a mixture of cooperation and discord reflecting the broad philosophical base of both groupings.

Nevertheless, it is true that the relationship has been typified by regular friction over the past two decades. This period coincides with the ideological polarization of the two organizations. Just as the Liberal Party moved to a full-blown neo-liberal agenda so ACOSS conclusively adopted opposing social democratic ideas. Consequently, much of the communication between ACOSS and the Liberals since the mid-1980s has been little more than a "dialogue of the deaf". However, both sides have elected to retain contact for pragmatic political purposes.

Whilst this ideological polarization had political consequences for both sides during the long period of Labor Party rule, it has had far greater implications for ACOSS since the Liberal Party regained government. In particular, ACOSS appears to have lost much of its effectiveness as an interest group as it enjoys little access to those policy networks which influence the policies and agendas of the Liberal-National Coalition Government. Not only has the Coalition government largely ignored

ACOSS' policy requests, but it has also actively sought to exclude ACOSS from policy debates.

ACOSS and the Liberal Party, Pre-1983

From its beginnings in 1956, ACOSS enjoyed a mixed, but sometimes fruitful relationship with the Liberal Party. For example, the Menzies Government provided ACOSS with its first government grant in 1966 which enabled the council to set up a Secretariat, and expand its activities. Regular contact was also maintained with leading public servants, and the Minister for Social Services. In general, ACOSS emphasized cooperation and consultation with the Liberal-National Coalition Governments of Menzies and his successors, rather than conflict or confrontation. However, relationships became more testy in the late 1960s when ACOSS began to criticize publicly government policies on issues such as social security payments, health insurance, and a national welfare inquiry.[1]

ACOSS retained contact with the Liberal Party Opposition from 1972–75, particularly through discussions with the Shadow Minister for Social Security, Don Chipp.[2] This dialogue appears to have influenced the Liberal Party towards substantially endorsing the expanded health and welfare programs introduced by the Labor Government. For example, the Liberal Party's 1975 federal election platform emphasized the need to "ensure that people are provided with a basic level of security below which no-one can involuntarily fall".[3]

The Liberal Party also criticized the 1975 government cuts to ACOSS' funding. Party leader Malcolm Fraser described the "slashing of funding for ACOSS . . . as evidence of Labor's unwillingness to tolerate competitors in the field of policy evaluation and formulation, and their ultimate preference for orderly, if ineffective bureaucratic mechanisms for dealing with what they like to think of as social welfare".[4] Similarly Liberal Party Senator Peter Baume condemned the cutting of funds from the "Councils of Social Service which have been instrumental in examining many of the welfare alternatives and programmes in Australia, and in promoting some decentralized policies emphasizing local control and movement of power away from Canberra".[5]

In contrast, ACOSS' relationship with the Fraser Coalition Government from 1975–83 was less agreeable. ACOSS was highly critical of government policies, and rarely balanced these criticisms with praise for government policies they supported. At times the government lost patience with what they considered to be ACOSS' confrontational and inflexible approach.

According to Margaret Guilfoyle, ACOSS were "always critical . . . they were always upping the ante on welfare expenditure. They didn't often suggest ways in which we could save welfare expenditure or prioritize".[6]

Nevertheless, the government granted ACOSS substantial access to key policy makers, including regular meetings with senior public servants, and with leading ministers. For example, ACOSS was included for the first ever time in 1982 in pre-budget discussions with the Prime Minister and Cabinet. Successive Social Security Ministers Margaret Guilfoyle and Fred Chaney, prominent social liberal Senator Peter Baume, and leading social policy bureaucrats worked cooperatively with ACOSS, and engaged in a complex exchange of policy ideas and strategies.

According to Chaney, "We believed ACOSS was broadly representative of the great range of organisations involved in the voluntary sector. Many of the grass-roots in these organisations were perhaps more conservative. For example, St Vincent de Paul and the Salvation Army, whilst deeply concerned with the plight of the poor, would generally be less political in their activities. ACOSS represented the activists, the politically committed element. I never thought they were not legitimate".[7] Baume remembered ACOSS as "an educated elite who articulated values of fairness and equity". Baume supported many of their objectives, and attempted to translate their concerns into language that would be acceptable to a non-labor government.[8] Overall there was always a group of social liberals who were willing to canvass ACOSS-type ideas within Liberal Party ranks.[9]

ACOSS and the Liberal Party, 1983–1996

Since 1983, however, the earlier complex and sometimes cooperative relationship between ACOSS and the Liberal Party seems to have come to an end. ACOSS' adoption of overt social democratic ideas based on increased government spending and higher taxation in order to reduce poverty rendered it less willing to seek or find common ground with a Liberal Party increasingly dominated by ideas of individualism and small government. In turn, many prominent Liberals accepted the argument of public choice theory that welfare lobbyists were self-interested individuals who should be excluded as far as possible from public policy debates. Conversely, those social liberals who favoured continued policy dialogue and cooperation with ACOSS found themselves progressively marginalized.

The relationship between ACOSS and the Liberal Party during the years of Labor Party rule can best be described as one of ideological confrontation and conflict. ACOSS voiced trenchant criticism of Liberal Party policies, which it regarded as unsympathetic to poor and disadvantaged Australians. ACOSS was particularly critical of proposed tax cuts for higher income earners, plans to reduce expenditure on social security payments, health and housing and other government programs and assistance, a suggestion to transfer all, or part of, the social security system to voluntary agencies, and the proposed introduction of a consumption tax within the Fightback package.[10] ACOSS also resented the Liberals' unwillingness to give adequate consideration to or to incorporate ACOSS' views into their policies.

The Liberals claimed in contrast that their policies were more likely to benefit the poor than were those of ACOSS. They had little time for ACOSS which they regarded as a "media machine rather than as a serious research and policy group".[11] They particularly resented ACOSS' tendency to focus much of its criticism on the Liberal Party, instead of concentrating its fire on the policies of the Labor Government. Liberal Shadow Ministers believed ACOSS had abandoned its traditional non-partisan political stance, and openly labelled the Council a Labor Party front. For example, Senator Richard Alston, then the Shadow Minister for Social Security, argued that ACOSS held "a simple-minded view of the ALP as the traditional party of social justice, and the Liberal Party as guilty until proven innocent".[12]

At the October 1991 ACOSS Congress the Liberal Party leader John Hewson delivered a stinging attack on ACOSS. Using public choice theory, Hewson claimed that ACOSS was more interested in obtaining more money for the welfare sector and in building large bureaucracies than in helping the poor. Hewson was particularly critical of ACOSS' attacks on Coalition plans to end unemployment benefits after nine months, and to partially privatize the Department of Social Security. He implied that ACOSS' criticism of the Liberals was biased and reflected its dependency on government funding. Hewson also criticized ACOSS for allegedly concentrating on improvements in social security payments instead of promoting broader employment and economic growth.[13]

According to a Liberal Party Shadow Minister, Hewson's speech "reflected the view in his office that the welfare lobby had had too much of a good thing for too long. There was a need to assess the direction and content of welfare. Hewson saw ACOSS as a bleeding hearts organization who were responsible for the bottomless pit of welfare expenditure".[14]

Another Liberal Party frontbencher Senator Richard Alston argued that Hewson's speech was a "calculated gamble. It was an attempt to try and reduce the power of one central organisation to purport to speak on behalf of a constituency. We were more interested in the views of those people at the coalface, rather than the professional activists . . . We didn't regard it as alienating the welfare sector. But, it certainly alienated the welfare professionals on the ACOSS Council".

Alston said that the Liberals had consulted with a wide range of welfare groups including the Salvation Army, the Brotherhood of St Laurence, Open Family, St Vincent de Paul, Sydney City Mission, and the Melbourne City Mission. According to Alston, they responded "pretty sympathetically. They regard ACOSS as looking for reasons to keep people out of the workforce and give more money to homeless kids. They don't believe you address the problem by throwing more money at them".[15]

ACOSS responded to Hewson's attack by arguing that, contrary to his assessment, it had devoted substantial attention to addressing the longer-term structural causes of poverty. In particular, ACOSS had developed policies on a wide range of issues which were designed to promote sustainable economic and employment growth. ACOSS also provided statistics to demonstrate that its own staff numbers and resources were extremely limited and hardly reflective of empire-building. ACOSS reaffirmed its commitment to a non-partisan political approach.[16]

Hewson's criticisms were also rebuffed by a number of leading welfare agencies and ACOSS affiliates including the Brotherhood of St Laurence, St Vincent de Paul, the Salvation Army, the Uniting Church and the Melbourne Wesley Central Mission. These agencies defended ACOSS' role in proposing policies which would promote economic development and create jobs. They criticized Hewson "for doing a serious injustice to an organisation which works to help some of the poorest and most disadvantaged people in this country".[17] Hewson subsequently threatened to cut ACOSS' government funding, querying whether ACOSS' policies actually served the interests of its constituency.[18]

Nevertheless despite the antagonism between the Liberal Party and ACOSS, regular contact between the two organizations still took place. Liberal leaders and Shadow Ministers were regularly invited to address ACOSS Congresses, and formal meetings between the Liberals and ACOSS also took place, even at the height of disagreements over the Fightback Package.

The significance of these meetings was that the Liberal Party was forced to recognize the political legitimacy and influence of ACOSS despite its disdain for interest groups in general and welfare lobby groups in particular. Commentators subsequently claimed that the Liberal Party's decision to exempt food from the proposed Goods and Services Tax represented a capitulation to pressure from ACOSS.[19]

Following the disastrous 1993 federal election loss, the Liberals attempted to rebuild bridges with ACOSS. In particular, the new Liberal Party leader, John Howard, actively praised ACOSS, and worked to restore relations. In his speech to the 1995 ACOSS Congress, he stated: "ACOSS plays a very important community role in raising public policy issues relevant to the needs and aspirations of the disadvantaged in our community. The people in this room are an important part of the glue which holds our society together". Howard added that "The Coalition Parties, under my leadership, are committed to a relationship of openness, good faith and a productive exchange of views with ACOSS".[20]

ACOSS and the Liberal-National Coalition Government, 1996–2006

Since the election of the Howard Government in March 1996, ACOSS and the Liberal Party have maintained a regular dialogue. During 2004–5, for example, ACOSS met with the Prime Minister, Treasurer, and two other key Ministers, plus representatives of major commonwealth departments and agencies.[21] Prime Minister Howard appears to have provided particularly good access to ACOSS.[22] However, it is arguably significant that this direct access to Ministers and their staff is no longer buttressed by membership of numerous government forums and advisory bodies such as the former Economic Planning Advisory Council as was the case during the Labor Government. Thus ACOSS appears to have less institutionalized opportunity than previously to influence the government's policy agenda.

Nevertheless, the major barrier to policy influence for ACOSS is arguably ideological, rather than structural. The dialogue between ACOSS and the Liberal Party is effectively paralyzed by the entrenched opposing views of the two sides. ACOSS continues to advocate a social democratic agenda including the retention of the welfare safety net, whereas the government remains wedded to a neo-liberal agenda of smaller government, lower taxation, and greater private provision of welfare. Consequently, ACOSS' influence on government policy has been at best insignificant. Most ACOSS proposals and criticisms of government policy have been rejected by the Government.[23]

However, both ACOSS and the government have had their own reasons for maintaining regular contact, and for publicly playing down the full extent of their differences. For ACOSS, regular access to government is based on the assumption that an insider lobbying strategy remains the best means of influencing government policy. On a number of occasions, the former ACOSS President Robert Fitzgerald emphasized the importance for consultation and advocacy purposes of retaining access to the Government unlike the Victorian Liberal Party Government which had completely excluded the community sector.[24] In short, ACOSS maintains that federal government policies would have been even worse for low income earners without ACOSS' intervention.[25]

Nevertheless, ACOSS seems to have little entree into the government's policy networks, whether they be political advisers, or bureaucrats, or party policy committees, or the Menzies Research Centre or external sources of consultation such as think tanks and business lobby groups. ACOSS did hold seminars in the early days of the new Government, designed to identify and illuminate the policy processes of the Liberal Party for the welfare sector.[26] However, these seminars appear to have had little influence. ACOSS has also attempted to appeal to the social justice and social liberal ideas espoused by Sir Robert Menzies, the founder of the Liberal Party, which assumed a role for the state in both intervening in the free market and protecting the poor.[27] However, as already noted, these ideas are currently marginal within the Liberal Party and government.

The only significant exception to this rule appears to be the Victorian backbencher, Petro Georgiou, who has publicly criticized the Howard Government's attacks on welfare recipients, and its failure to incorporate the Liberal Party's traditional concern for social justice into its welfare policies.[28] Georgiou's dissent from government policies was heartily welcomed by ACOSS,[29] but met with only a telling silence from the Government. Other dissenters such as Judi Moylan have also struggled to make a serious impact on social policy debates.[30]

For the Government, regular contact with ACOSS arguably serves as a means of pacifying, or at least negotiating with, a potentially critical, or even damaging, interest group. And this dialogue should be considered not in isolation, but rather within the broader context of the government's campaign to exclude and marginalize welfare advocacy groups. Influenced by public choice theory which depicts welfare advocacy groups as manipulating the redistributive process to their own advantage,[31] this campaign has had a number of different manifestations.

The most overt form has been the outright de-funding of 15 major peak welfare bodies including the Australian Pensioners and Superannuants Federation, the Australian Community Health Association, National Shelter, the Australian Youth Policy Action Coalition, the Association of Civilian Widows, Family Planning Australia, and the Australian Catholic Social Welfare Commission family planning division.[32]

An associated initiative has been the attempt by the Government to silence, or at least restrain, organized expressions of dissent from those peak bodies which retain funding. For example, the government issued a statement in August 1999 requesting that funded bodies work collaboratively with the Department of Family and Community Services, and provide early warning for all controversial issues planned for media coverage, and which might attract public comment. This request appeared designed to muzzle funded bodies by reducing them to agents of government, rather than autonomous vehicles for community participation in policy development and decision-making.[33]

In addition, the Treasurer Peter Costello released a draft Charities Bill which community welfare organizations criticized as containing unreasonable and unnecessary restrictions on the advocacy role of charities. The Bill was clearly influenced by public choice assumptions, and threatened to remove tax exemptions and concessions from organizations whose purpose is deemed to be "attempting to change the law or government policy" if such action is "more than ancillary or incidental to their core purpose". The Bill appeared to be aimed at silencing charities such as the Brotherhood of St Laurence and St Vincent de Paul which both provide direct welfare services, and advocate changes in government policy.[34] However, the Treasurer eventually announced an indefinite deferral of the Bill.

In a further development, the government funded the neo-liberal think tank, the Institute of Public Affairs (IPA), to audit non-government organizations including ACOSS regarding their relationship with government departments. This audit provoked some concern given that the IPA is driven by public choice assumptions, and has a long-standing animus against both the welfare state and welfare lobby groups. The IPA report recommended the introduction of a series of protocols designed to expose the allegedly overbearing influence of NGOs on government decision-making processes.[35]

The Government also committed $50,000 to develop a new Not-for-Profit Council of Australia which would act as a single voice for all community groups, not just welfare bodies and charities. Many viewed the proposal as an attempt to marginalize or replace ACOSS as the peak representative of the community welfare sector.[36]

All these initiatives suggest a concern to silence or at least tame and co-opt welfare advocacy groups. Some groups are openly bullied or de-funded, whilst others such as ACOSS are handled with greater caution. Noticeably in contrast to the former Liberal Party leader, John Hewson, Prime Minister Howard has not openly denounced ACOSS as a self-interested lobby group, or threatened to cut its government funding. On the contrary, Howard has often praised ACOSS, and emphasized his commitment to ongoing dialogue with the Council despite differences of opinion.[37] The government has also confirmed ACOSS' ongoing funding grant.[38]

Howard's mixed approach to ACOSS is almost certainly influenced by the prominence within the Council of the key non-government charities such as the Salvation Army and St Vincent de Paul that he personally greatly admires. At least in part, Howard recognizes ACOSS' lobbying activities as representing the legitimate public policy concerns of those who work privately with the disadvantaged at the "coalface".[39]

This means that Howard may be reluctant for political and personal reasons to completely marginalize ACOSS which simultaneously represents for the government both bad sectional interests, and those private charities whom Howard wishes to involve further in both policy making and service provision. However, this does not preclude the Government from attempting to split ACOSS down the middle by hiving off the large private charities, many of whom are now dependent on the Government for tender income, from the so-called professional lobbyists. This has long been an aim of the Liberal Party, and the rise to public prominence of Patrick McClure, the CEO of Mission Australia (as Chair of the government's Reference Group on Welfare Reform and now a member of the Fair Pay Commission) suggests that this strategy is beginning to take shape.

The government has also launched some direct frontal attacks on ACOSS. For example, the Prime Minister responded to ACOSS criticisms of the government's taxation package by suggesting that ACOSS was just another interest group which was not even representative of the whole welfare sector.[40] Threats were also made to politically punish and marginalize ACOSS for its critical stance on taxation should the Coalition win the 1998 federal election.[41] Later Howard again attacked ACOSS, suggesting that its opposition to government tax policies was not serving the best interests of the poor.[42]

Further criticism came from the Employment Services Minister Tony Abbott who rebuked ACOSS for criticizing the Job Network. Abbott claimed there was a split in ACOSS between "people willing to work in the system and people like ACOSS President Michael Raper with their old-style Left ideologies".[43] And the Minister for Family & Community Services Amanda Vanstone accused ACOSS of "misleading the public" by releasing allegedly incorrect estimates of welfare breaching penalties. Indeed, Vanstone asserted threateningly that "agencies that are publicly funded to sponsor responsible debate need to check that their information is right".[44]

The evidence suggests that ACOSS has been increasingly marginalized since the 1998 federal election. Despite ACOSS' central role in the taxation debate, no ACOSS representative was appointed to the Government's Tax Consultative Committee announced in November 1998, nor to the New Tax System Advisory Board announced in August 1999 or the associated Community Sector Advisory Panel. In addition, the October 1999 Senate Inquiry into business tax reform did not seek any representations from the welfare sector. Even more notably, the government chose not to appoint any

ACOSS representative to the Reference Group on Welfare Reform despite ACOSS' key role in the welfare policy debate, nor was ACOSS granted a representative on the Welfare Reform Consultative Forum.

Conclusion

Historically, ACOSS has enjoyed a mixed association with the Liberal Party. During the Menzies era and subsequent Fraser years, the intra-organizational relationship ranged from one of mutual cooperation and cross-fertilization of ideas, to one of harsh criticism. Yet in general, Liberal-National Coalition Governments were sufficiently pluralistic and pragmatic to listen to and sometimes adopt significant aspects of ACOSS policy.

However, the current Liberal Party appears to be unequivocally committed to neo-liberal ideas, and the retrenchment of the welfare state. It has adopted a highly narrow rather than inclusive approach to policy development, and seems unwilling to tolerate alternative sources of advice within its own policy network. The Liberals are highly suspicious of welfare advocacy groups, and seem to regard ACOSS as little more than an open ally of the Labor Party.

To be sure, ACOSS has continued to pronounce its political bipartisanship, and to retain an ongoing dialogue with the government. But the evidence suggests that access to the current government for ACOSS no longer correlates with genuine policy influence.

Questions for Discussion

➤ Have ACOSS and the Liberal Party always been "political enemies"?

➤ What are some of the key factors that have contributed to the conflict between ACOSS and the Liberal Party?

➤ Discuss the relationship between ACOSS and the current Liberal-National Coalition Government.

8

A Natural Alliance?

The relationship between the Australian Trade Union movement and the Australian Council of Social Service

Over the past two decades, trade unions (which claim to represent the working class including the working poor) and the welfare lobby (which claims to represent the poor and disadvantaged whether employed or social security recipients) have increasingly collaborated on matters of common concern. As a result, some commentators have argued the existence of a "natural alliance" between the two groupings.[1]

The assumption underlying such an alliance is that trade unions and the welfare lobby are the two interest groups most committed to a social democratic agenda. By social democratic, I mean a commitment to substantial government intervention in the economy and a wide-ranging welfare state to alleviate market-based inequality and ensure minimum standards of support for all citizens. In political terms, united pressure from unions and welfare would arguably be central to influencing a future Labor Party Government in a social democratic direction. And in the current unfavourable political climate, united pressure from the unions and welfare is equally important for resisting the neo-liberal campaign to simultaneously cut wages and working conditions and welfare entitlements.

Yet despite the considerable political and ideological common ground between the two sectors, such an alliance has not always proceeded smoothly in the past. The principal obstacle to more effective collaboration has been that the economic interests of the workers (including well-paid workers) have not always proven to be the same as the interests of the poor. In addition, the narrow labourism of the union movement based on wage protection rather than broader social democratic concepts has tended to mitigate against such an alliance.

However, the argument of this chapter is that an alliance based on broader political and strategic (rather than narrowly defined economic) interests is more likely to be successful. Such a coalition of interest may at times be based on a formal joint framework or affiliation, and at other times be more flexibly and informally directed at particular areas of common interest.

The Labourism of the Australian Union Movement

The Australian union movement's attitude to welfare issues and the welfare sector can best be explained by reference to its labourist tradition. Labourism emerged from the indirect, pragmatic representation of craft unions at the parliamentary level. The principal focus of labourism was to secure the wages and working conditions of male workers, rather than social rights for all citizens.[2] Only limited emphasis was placed on a broader redistribution of income that alters the basic structural inequities between rich and poor.

This labourist philosophy has generally paid little attention to the needs of those who do not participate in the workforce, except for the sick and the aged.[3] During the 1930s Depression, for example, the union movement, whilst expressing sympathy for the unemployed, with some exceptions, generally made little attempt to organize the unemployed or to lobby on their behalf for adequate unemployment relief. As noted by historian, L. J. Louis, unemployed workers quickly became isolated from the mainstream union movement.[4]

However, in the mid-late 1960s, the rediscovery of poverty by welfare groups, academic researchers, and the popular media encouraged the union movement to begin considering broader social policy issues. In 1969, Bob Hawke was elected President of the Australian Council of Trade Unions (ACTU). Hawke immediately declared his intention to develop policies beyond the traditional areas of wages and working conditions. Hawke said that the union movement would intervene in "anything that constitutes discrimination or hardship against our people".[5]

Under Hawke's Presidency, the union movement involved itself in a number of broader social and political issues not directly related to employment conditions. These included the green bans of the Builders Labourers Federation, the first ever national strike over Medibank in 1976, strikes against the mining and export of uranium, the work bans on the Newport power station, and the ban on drilling at Noonkanbah in Western Australia in support of the Aborigines.[6] Influenced by the Henderson Poverty Inquiry which drew attention to the link between low wages and poverty, the ACTU also undertook some research into social policy issues.

During the Fraser Government years, the union movement promulgated the notion of the social wage: that standards of living are affected by far more than just private incomes received by individuals through wages and salaries and non-wage benefits. The movement argued that government spending on goods and services, such as education, health, social security and welfare, and housing and community amenities, was just as important.

The social wage campaign reflected the growth of unemployment and its detrimental impact on union strength. Large numbers of union members were not only forced to survive on social security benefits, but also ceased to pay their union dues and/or terminated their involvement with the movement. In response, the union movement developed a political strategy that was designed not only to protect the immediate economic interests of the unemployed and employed via increasing the social wage, but also to buttress the overall strength of the union movement by promoting policies that would hopefully reduce unemployment and so reverse the decline in union membership.[7]

The ultimate creation of the trade union social wage campaign was the 1983 Australian Labor Party/ACTU Accord. The Accord endorsed "a fairer taxation system and social wage involving increased provision by the government of health, education, housing and social welfare services".[8] The Accord promised to "address anomalies in welfare coverage; to foster social equity by striving to improve the relative position of the most disadvantaged; to take urgent action to restore the position of the recipients of unemployment benefits; and to develop automatic indexation provisions (and restoration of the relative value of pensions) to the basic rate of 25 per cent of average male earnings").[9]

Most importantly, the Accord recognized "the inherent limits to improvements in the existing welfare system, and the need to develop new alternatives less subject to the vagaries of the annual Budget process and conservative cost-cutting".[10] This passage suggested that the union movement might finally include social security claims as part of its annual wages submission. However, this did not happen and welfare payments remained vulnerable to the economic rationalist approach which characterized the policies of both major parties.[11] Alongside the formal Accord process, the ACTU continued to promote the interests of social security beneficiaries in various other submissions and statements, and was particularly active in promoting the introduction of the Family Allowance Supplement.[12]

Nevertheless, whilst there is little doubt that the union movement has viewed low income and disadvantaged Australians as part of its constituency and on occasions actively lobbied for their interests, there is equally little doubt that this lobbying has been secondary to the movement's prime aim of representing the immediate interests of its members. In general, the ACTU did not challenge or protest spending cuts by the Hawke/Keating Labor Party Governments which hurt and disadvantaged low income earners. And equally the ACTU has rarely been active in protesting the Howard Coalition Government's retrenchment of income security payments and entitlements. In short, the movement has arguably remained wedded to a narrow labourist, rather than social democratic definition, of its constituency.

ACOSS and the Trade Unions, 1956–2006

Prior to the Fraser Government years, there was little contact between ACOSS and the union movement. As already discussed, the union movement with its labourist emphasis on wage rates and employment conditions displayed limited interest in social welfare payments or the rights of social security recipients. Since unemployment was at a low level during most of this period, few unionists experienced the poverty faced by those dependent on the social security system.

Equally, ACOSS displayed little interest in joint action with the union movement. According to long-time ACOSS Chairman, Major-General Gordon, "We had no relationship at all with the trade union movement. We limited our work to the members of our organization. The trade union movement didn't join us and it never occurred to us to approach them because they were in a different field".[13]

Nevertheless, some contact between the organizations did take place. As early as January 1956, the Provisional Executive of the Australian Social Welfare Council (ASWC) approached the ACTU for a statement of Trade Union Welfare Services to be included in a report to an international welfare conference.[14] Then in November 1956, the ASWC voted to invite the ACTU to become a member of the Council. The reason for this invitation was concern that the Council would be outflanked by the government's proposed Welfare Advisory Committee to which the ACTU had been invited to contribute a representative.[15] However, the ACTU rejected the invitation.

Four years later, the Queensland Council of Social Service requested permission to invite the local Trades Hall Council to become an affiliate. The ACOSS Executive responded that State Councils of Social Service were free to make their own decisions in respect to membership.[16] In 1966, ACOSS voted to approach the leaders of industry and the trade union movement in an attempt to attain their financial support through membership of either an appropriate State Council, or via associate membership of ACOSS, and/or by offering donations to ACOSS and the local State Councils.[17] It is unclear whether the approaches were successful. That same year a prominent ACOSS activist, Anglican Bishop Geoffrey Sambell, expressed his concern at the lack of involvement of trade unions and their members in community welfare services and planning.[18]

The first significant link between ACOSS and trade unions appears to have emerged in 1970 when ACTU President Bob Hawke and two representatives from the Australian Council of Salaried and Professional Associations addressed the Sixth National Conference of ACOSS on the topic of "The Trade Unions and Social Welfare".[19] The union interest in ACOSS reflected the growing public and labour movement concern with poverty, as provoked by the Henderson Report on poverty in Victoria. Equally, ACOSS' growing interest in welfarist and even social democratic ideas led it to value a closer association with the trade union movement.[20]

Further meetings between ACOSS and the ACTU were held during the Whitlam Government years to discuss common concerns such as the Australian Assistance Plan, a cooperative regional participatory social planning program formulated by the Social Welfare Commission which envisaged the creation of new local governing bodies, Regional Councils for Social Development, to coordinate and advise on matters of social welfare.[21] Individual ACTU officials such as Ralph Willis also participated in ACOSS policy committees. Nevertheless, such cooperation remained limited and informal. According to ACOSS President David Scott who spoke at the ACTU Summer School in 1974/75, the union movement held a "fairly simplistic view" that following the introduction of centralized welfare services by a Labor Government the non-government sector should just "wither away".[22]

During the Fraser Government years, ACOSS established stronger and more organized links with the union movement.[23] The union movement's interest in ACOSS reflected its growing concern with the issue of unemployment and the financial impact on its retrenched members. ACOSS' interest in links with the union movement reflected its growing sympathy for social democratic ideas, and its concern to form alliances against the policies of the Fraser Government.

At times, ACOSS' agenda was far narrower, and it often seemed to merely bracket the union movement with the Business Council of Australia as a potential means of financial support. Nevertheless, ACOSS/ACTU dialogue addressed a number of issues including unemployment, legal aid, Medibank, and social security payments, and a joint ACOSS/ACTU Action Committee was formed to promote ACOSS' "Work Together" campaign on unemployment.[24] In addition, ACTU representative Alan Matheson was active in the ACOSS Immigration, Integration and Population Committee.

ACOSS also formed links with white collar unions such as the Australian Council of Salaried and Professional Associations (ACSPA) and the Clerical and Administrative Government Employers Organization (CAGEO). However, ACOSS rejected approaches from the public sector unions and the left-wing Amalgamated Metal Workers and Shipwrights Union (AMWSU) to join broader anti-government political campaigns due to concern at their partisan political nature.[25]

Overall cooperation between the two sectors continued to be ad hoc. Former ACOSS staffer Joan McLintock recalls being very critical of the views of unions at one joint meeting on unemployment: "It was the most incredible eye-opener. The attitudes of individual union representatives to the unemployed were abysmal. It was as simplistic as saying we would virtually make sure that any son of a unionist got a job".[26]

During the Hawke/Keating Labor Government years, ACOSS developed a stronger, more formal working relationship with the union movement. Yet, this relationship remained too fitful and inconsistent to be designated a formal alliance. Certainly on some issues such as opposition to a proposed consumption tax, support for social security reforms such as the Family Allowance Supplement, and addressing youth unemployment, ACOSS and the ACTU acted in close alliance.[27] However, on other issues such as tax cuts and superannuation, ACOSS and the ACTU sat on opposite sides. What was most noteworthy was not that the interests of the ACOSS and ACTU constituencies often converged, but rather the fact that on other occasions their interests sharply diverged.

To be sure, ACOSS and the ACTU broadly agreed on most issues. Cooperation was particularly effective on opposition to privatization of public services and cuts to welfare spending.[28] For example, ACOSS combined with public sector unions and welfare groups to place advertisements in every major metropolitan daily protesting proposed Budget cuts to welfare expenditure and the social wage.[29] ACOSS also participated in the New Visions Alliance alongside the ACTU and seven other national peak bodies.[30] ACTU representatives regularly spoke at ACOSS Congresses, and an ACTU representative, Sharan Burrow, participated in the Future of Work Commission established by ACOSS.

Yet, welfare advocates continued to express concern that the union movement's agenda was limited by its adherence to the Accord, and its prioritizing of the wage claims of its comparatively highly-paid members over the concerns of lower paid workers and the unemployed.[31] Former ACOSS Director Mark Lyons stated bluntly: "We are not natural allies. There is something to be said for Frank Castles view of Australian history that the trade union movement has been on balance a bad thing, rather than a good thing for low income people (people who can't get jobs), and it did seem at times that their interest was significantly and primarily their work membership".[32]

This divergence of interests was characterized most strongly by disagreements over the issue of the ALP Government's superannuation scheme. ACOSS campaigned vigorously against the scheme, claiming that the tax concessions were inequitable in that they favoured higher income earners at the expense of people with lower disposable incomes.[33] In contrast, the ACTU remained a strong supporter of the scheme.[34]

Former ACOSS President Julian Disney called the ACTU's approach to superannuation "an outrageous episode of selfishness, both the issue and the way they treated us".[35] But ACTU President Martin Ferguson argued that "ACOSS have an unrealistic understanding of the nature of the Industrial Relations System and what's possible through the Arbitration Commission and negotiations with employers. They say that the Superannuation Guarantee is taking money away from low-paid workers. They don't understand the Commission is not going to give these low-paid workers a wage increase".

Ferguson added: "ACOSS is respected as being a voice for the underprivileged in the community, for the unemployed and young people in need. But they are not always regarded as practical. We believe you can't always get what you want. We tend to be a bit pragmatic and are more capable of working out our priorities and getting the most urgent need, whereas ACOSS tend to go for the ultimate position on everything".[36]

Since the election of the Coalition Government in March 1996, ACOSS and the ACTU have tended to minimize their differences whilst forging a common opposition to government policies. The new ACTU President Jennie George saw ACOSS as a natural ally of the union movement, and encouraged stronger links between the two organizations.[37]

Shortly before the election of the Coalition Government, for example, a combined ACOSS-ACTU delegation toured New Zealand to examine the social and economic impact of the New Zealand Government's free market reforms. Particular attention was drawn to the perceived connection between the deregulation of the labour market, and the cuts to welfare benefits. The delegation concluded that it would be economically and socially risky for Australia to follow the reforms which had contributed to increased levels of inequality and poverty.[38] ACOSS and the ACTU also co-commissioned a study of the distributional impact of the 1996–97 Federal Budget.

The study found that the Budget had left most households worse-off – with low-income people hit the hardest.[39]

ACOSS has increasingly recognized the link between wages and welfare, and the likelihood that decreased minimum wages will be accompanied by reduced income security payments. This recognition has led ACOSS to support the ACTU's opposition to government proposals to weaken wages and working conditions. For example, ACOSS joined the ACTU in opposing the Liberal/National Coalition's initial industrial relations reforms on the basis that they would hurt low-income workers.[40] ACOSS also intervened for the first ever time in a major national wage case to support the ACTU's call for a significant wage rise for low-paid workers. In its submission to the Australian Industrial Relations Commission, ACOSS argued that wages and welfare policies were closely connected, and that the interests of income security recipients and low wage earning households are "one and the same".[41] Subsequent ACOSS submissions on wages have urged similar outcomes.[42]

The union movement has welcomed ACOSS' support for higher minimum wages, and a number of union representatives have contributed to ACOSS forums and publications.[43] ACOSS has also collaborated with a number of trade unions in broad alliances such as Australian Collaboration and Services First.

For and Against: "A Natural Alliance"

Both the welfare sector and the union movement can identify potential gains from a closer alliance. From the viewpoint of ACOSS, closer cooperation with the ACTU offers the potential of support for social welfare objectives from an influential and powerful lobby group. For example, it is unlikely that ACOSS alone could resist or dissuade a conservative Government committed to a substantial contraction of the welfare state. However, it is possible that the union movement (backed by ACOSS) would have the power to initiate the combative strategy necessary to alter or change such an agenda.

From the viewpoint of the unions, closer cooperation with ACOSS and other social movements also appeals in that it offers a broadening of the union movement's own dwindling base of support.[44] This is particularly important in the current political climate whereby the ACTU is able to exert little influence on the policies of the Coalition Government.[45] ACOSS' intervention in support of the ACTU's "Living Wage" claim provides a concrete example of the potential gains for the unions from a closer alliance.

However, mutually beneficial movement towards a tighter or "natural" alliance arguably depends on the union movement's capacity to abandon its traditional labourism in favour of the adoption of a broader social democratic agenda. Under the currently existing circumstances, the ACTU and ACOSS may continue to enter into tactical alliances from time to time, but any broader alliance is likely to be circumscribed by notions of economic self-interest. Whilst a labourist union movement may claim to represent the needs of all low income earners including the ACOSS membership, the limitations of labourism are in practice likely to prevent the unions from adequately representing the political interests of this larger constituency.

Consequently, the narrow economic interests of these two different – albeit sometimes overlapping – constituencies will not always be the same. Sometimes, they may come into direct conflict, as is the case when limited government spending can be applied to tax cuts or welfare increases, but not to both. Alternatively, the ACTU may prioritize the wage demands of more influential higher paid workers at the expense of low-paid workers. Reasonable wage gains for middle and high income union members are not necessarily compatible with either greater overall equality, or the availability of greater resources to combat poverty.

The alternative social democratic strategy would mean the ACTU articulating working class political interests independently of narrow economic interests. This would mean the union movement making a commitment to the political mobilization of non-workers (particularly the currently disenfranchised unemployed) instead of just its wage-earning membership, and would require a radical break with its history and ideological framework. It would mean the union movement prioritizing social democratic strategies involving redistribution of income and greater overall equity, rather than the narrow wage claims of employed unionists. In addition, ACOSS would need to adopt a more strategic approach to lobbying government based on a broader definition of its constituency's interests. This could include subsuming on occasions the particular interests of low income earners to a broader social democratic or pragmatic political agenda.

All possible scenarios suggest that whilst there is significant common ground for ACOSS and the ACTU to collaborate on issues of mutual concern, any mutual action should be based on the continued organizational and campaign independence of the two parties.

Conclusion

This analysis indicates that there are some difficulties with the concept of a "natural alliance" between the unions and the welfare lobby, particularly one based on the assumption of union leadership or domination. Nevertheless, the continuing divergence between the economic self-interest of the respective constituencies does not in itself preclude the possibilities for a broader alliance, particularly if the union movement is able to move towards a broader social democratic definition of its political constituency and interests.

On the contrary, the ongoing debate around minimum wages (and its potential implications for welfare payments) suggests that the unions and welfare groups possess similar strategic interests. The involvement of ACOSS in the "Living Wage" campaign and the active encouragement of such involvement by the ACTU suggests that this commonality of interest to prevent the development of a larger group of "working poor" is already understood.

Whilst such an alliance may take different forms depending on particular political contexts and objectives, it does appear that the ACTU and ACOSS will continue to work closely together both on specific issues and campaigns, and more broadly to promote social democratic ideas about greater social and economic equality.

Questions for Discussion

➤ Why is it often assumed that ACOSS and the trade union movement are "natural allies"?

➤ Are the interests of union members necessarily the same as those of welfare consumers?

➤ How does ACOSS interpret the link between wage policies and income security policies?

Conclusion

ACOSS has existed as a unique organization for 50 years representing both the concerns of its mainly welfare service provider membership, and the broader interests of low income and disadvantaged Australians. During this period, it has confronted and overcome a number of organizational, ideological, political and resource challenges.

Some examples of ACOSS' historical achievements include ensuring the adequate representation of welfare consumers within the Council's decision-making structure; achieving an ideological consensus on key policy issues and speaking with a united and representative voice in its public presentations; implementing a range of effective lobbying strategies; maintaining an on-going dialogue with all mainstream political parties and other key interest groups; developing a high public and media profile in social policy debates; and securing sufficient resources to successfully undertake its core activities.

Specific policy reforms or outcomes influenced by ACOSS lobbying have included: the 1963 increase in payments to civilian widows; the 1969 health care reforms introduced by the Gorton Coalition Government and the later introduction of Medibank by the Whitlam ALP Government; the establishment of the Henderson Poverty Inquiry by the McMahon Coalition Government and the subsequent broadening of that inquiry by the ALP; the introduction of the Supporting Mothers Pension by the Whitlam Government; the expansion of interpreter and other migrant support services in the early to mid 1970s; the easing of harsh invalid pension criteria introduced by the Fraser Coalition Government; the establishment of Welfare Rights Centres; the Family Assistance Package of 1987; the defeat of the Coalition's proposed consumption tax in 1993; and more recently the softening of the Howard Government's harsh breaching legislation.

ACOSS has achieved these positive outcomes despite some obvious limitations including the general powerlessness of its core poor and disadvantaged constituency, the highly diverse character of its membership, the difficulty of maintaining a bipartisan party political position in a highly polarized political environment, the long-term domination of economic rationalist ideas, and the associated pressure on advocacy groups to either cease public dissent or lose government funding.

ACOSS is likely to face similar challenges in the future. For example, the domination of economic rationalist discourse which privileges economic growth and wealth creation over social well-being and income redistribution is likely to continue for the foreseeable future. A related development is the rise of economic globalization which is widely perceived as reducing the capacity of national governments to undertake generous social spending. And an additional potential long-term hurdle is posed by Australia's ageing population which is already being used as an excuse by the Coalition Government (as canvassed in the 2002 Intergenerational Report) to limit social spending in a number of areas.[1]

The priorities for ACOSS appear to be threefold: firstly to reframe social problems in language that encourages public opinion to sympathize with allegedly less "deserving" disadvantaged groups such as the unemployed, sole parents and indigenous Australians. At present, the Coalition Government is generously directing significant resources towards so-called deserving groups such as low-income nuclear families and the aged, whilst acting punitively towards other groups as reflected in the Welfare to Work Bill.[2] ACOSS needs to challenge this discrimination by developing strategies that effectively reconnect the lives and experiences of all disadvantaged groups with mainstream society.

An associated task for ACOSS is to find the energy and resources to be pro-active in articulating progressive alternatives to the dominant economic rationalist agenda rather than simply trying to defend what is left of the traditional welfare state. At the very least, ACOSS should be arguing for a more bottom-up welfare system based on a genuine partnership between the state, welfare consumers, and the community. Within such a model, welfare services would be driven by the needs and rights of service users rather than by those of government and service providers.[3]

A final priority is for ACOSS to form new alliances from the local to the regional to the global that provide effective political structures for implementing such alternatives. Given the increasing influence of global economic pressures and policy actors on national policy debates, it is imperative that ACOSS participate in movements for global justice based on introducing programs for taxation and redistribution similar to those existing at the national level. Broadly this means aiming at the development of an international welfare state that sets binding social standards. And more specifically, ACOSS has an interest in resourcing and assisting the profile of regional non-government organizations as a means of lifting social welfare standards throughout the region.[4]

Appendices

Appendix I: ACOSS Leaders

ACOSS Presidents

1956–1957: Reverend Darcy O'Reilly – Methodist Church and New South Wales Council of Social Service
1957– 1961: Professor Morven Brown – Schools of Social Work
1961–1964: Dr John Hunter – Australian Medical Association
1964–1971: Major-General Roy Gordon – Services Canteens Trust Fund
1971–1973: Judith Green – New South Wales Council of Social Service
1973–1977: David Scott – Brotherhood of St Laurence
1977–1979: Peter Travers – South Australian Catholic Family Welfare Bureau
1979–1981: Murray Geddes – Lecturer and Consultant
1981–1985: Bruce McKenzie – Warnambool Institute of Advanced Education
1985–1989: Julian Disney – Welfare Rights Centre
1989–1993: Merle Mitchell – Springvale Community Aid and Advice Bureau
1993–1997: Robert Fitzgerald – St Vincent de Paul NSW
1997–2001: Michael Raper – Welfare Rights Centre
2001–2005: Andrew McCallum – St Luke's Bendigo
2005–2006: Lin Hatfield Dodds – Uniting Care Australia

ACOSS Directors

1970–1974: Joan Brown
1974–1975: Edward Pennington
1975–1976: Joan McLintock
1976–1980: Ian Yates
1980–1983: Joan McLintock

1983–1985:	Colin Menzies
1985–1989:	Mark Lyons
1989–1994:	Garth Noweland-Foreman
1994–2001:	Betty Hounslow
2001–2004:	Megan Mitchell
2005–2006:	Andrew Johnson

Appendix II: ACOSS Publications

ACOSS Journals and Newsletters

ACOSS Annual Reports, 1956–2005.
ACOSS Action, 1975–1983.
ACOSS Quarterly, 1964–1970.
Australian Journal of Social Issues, 1967–2006.
Australian Social Welfare/Impact, 1971–2006
Community Tax Newsletter, 1985.
Corporate Associates Newsletter, 1981–1982.
Equity, 1985–1989.
Work Together News, 1979.

ACOSS Publications

Proceedings of First National Conference of Social Welfare, 1960.
Proceedings of the Second National Conference, 1962.
Widows in Australia, 1962.
Social Progress Through Social Planning, 1964.
Terminology Project. International Conference of Social Work, 1965.
The National Income and Social Welfare, 1965.
Community Service: Citizens and Social Welfare Organizations, 1966.
Some Issues in Social Policy with Special Reference to the Role of ACOSS, 1967.
Survey of Voluntary Agencies, Victoria, 1965–1967, 1968.
Submission to the Commonwealth Committee of Enquiry into Health Insurance, 1968.
Ethnic Minorities in Australia, 1968.
Social Welfare and Human Rights, 1968.
Submission to the Commonwealth Government for Financial Support for Three Year Period – July 1969 to June, 1972, 1969.
Submission to the Standing Committee on Health and Welfare, 1970.

Appendices

Submission to the Minister for Social Services on Aspects of Social Service Benefits which Merit Attention in the 1970–71 Commonwealth Budget, 1970.

New Town Forum, 1970.

Workshop on The Rehabilitation of the Psychiatrically Ill amongst the Migrant Population, 1970.

Focus on Migrants, 1970.

New Strategies for Social Development – The Role of Social Welfare, 1970.

Aspects of Social Service Benefits which Merit Attention in the Commonwealth Budget 1971–72, 1971.

Proceedings of the 1st National Family and Child Welfare Conference, 1971.

The Single Parent Family in Australia, 1972.

The Family in Australia: Towards A National Policy, 1972.

Social Welfare for Fatherless Families, 1972.

Constitution, 1972.

The Making of Social Policy, 1972.

Aspects of Social Service Benefits which Merit Attention in the Commonwealth Budget 1972–73, 1972.

Proceedings of Annual Meeting of the Australian Council of Social Service, 1972.

Social Welfare Education in Australia, 1973.

Social Welfare Consequences of Change, 1973.

Poverty: The ACOSS Evidence, 1973.

Submission to the Commonwealth Taxation Review Committee, 1973.

Foster Care in Australia, 1973.

Submission for Increased Support to ACOSS by the Commonwealth Government, 1973.

National Compensation and Rehabilitation, 1973.

Action for Social Change: Whose Responsibility? 1974.

Family Law Bill, 1974.

Some Developments in ACOSS Policies, 1974.

Homemaker and Homehelp Services in Australia, 1974.

Australian Population Policies, 1974.

Participation in Australia, 1974.

ACOSS Study On Landlord/Tenant Relations, 1974.

Statement on Social Security Benefits and Related Matters, 1974.

Family Welfare, 1974.

Are We Second Class Citizens? 1974.

The Australian Assistance Plan: A Pilot Program in Social Planning. Prepared for the ICSW Regional Conference for Asia and Western Pacific, 1975.

Human Relationships in Australia, 1975.

Assistance to Industry, 1975.

The Philosophy of the Bill – Compensation and Rehabilitation in Australia, 1975.

Budget Demands, 1975.

Australian Budget Process, 1975.

ACOSS Still Fights For A Fair Grant, 1975.

Guaranteed Minimum Income. Towards the Development of a Policy, 1975.

Seminar on Guaranteed Minimum Income, 1975.
Partnership or Paternalism? 1975.
ACOSS Action Campaign, 1975.
Social Security Benefits and Related Matters, 1975.
Agenda for Action, 1975.
Social Policies for Australia: The ACOSS Programme Planning Prospectus, 1975.
Survival Kit: Project Profiles and Submissions, 1975.
Community Funding, 1976.
Welfare Priorities for the Commonwealth Budget 1976/77, 1976.
Suggested Changes in ACOSS Objects as set out in its Constitution, 1976.
Immigrants and Mental Health, 1976.
Unemployment – Facts and Fallacies, 1976.
Submission on the Care of the Aged and Infirm, 1976.
The Future of Legal Aid or Guilty Until Proved Wealthy? 1976.
Submission to the Review of the Commonwealth Employment Service, 1976.
People Not Blueprints, 1976.
Submission to Medibank Review Committee, 1976.
Budget Perspectives, 1976.
Equal Opportunity in Australia, 1976.
Unemployment – Who and Why, 1977.
The Unemployed: Welfare or Justice? 1977.
Lone Parent Forum. Equality Without Discrimination, 1977.
Whatever Happened to Full Employment? 1977.
Real Reform or a Sideways Shuffle, 1977.
Unemployment, Its Costs and Casualties, 1977.
Workless or Worthless? 1977.
Welfare Under Challenge, 1977.
Submission to the Commonwealth Government for 1977–78 Grants, 1977.
Freedom of Information, 1978.
Joint Emergency Relief Study, 1978.
Background on ACOSS Private Sector Approach, 1978.
Emergency Relief – A Study of Agencies and Clients, 1978.
Review of ACOSS Roles, Functions, Methods of Operation, and Finance, 1978.
Submission on Freedom of Information Bill, 1978.
Means Testing and Social Welfare Policy, 1978.
Adjusting to Change, 1978.
Chance or Choice, 1978.
Australian Background Papers on Human Well-Being, 1978.
Budget 78/79: A Budget With High Costs, 1978.
Policy and Practice, 1978.
The Self-Help Movement in Australia, 1979.
Social Security Appeals, 1979.
Intercountry Adoption and Sponsorship, 1979.
Australian Non-government sector tomorrow, 1979.
Who Wins, Who Loses? People's Welfare: The Commonwealth Budget Priority in 1979–80, 1979.

Business and the Social Fabric, 1980.
Corporate Associates Program, 1980.
Submission to the Australian Financial System Inquiry, 1980.
Report of Proceedings of Seminar on Tax Reform and Social Welfare, 1980.
Early Retirement: Blessing or Curse, 1980.
Facts on Welfare, 1980.
Future of ACOSS Under Threat, 1980.
More or Less Health: The Jamison Report, 1981.
Share the Health, 1981.
Through the Hoops, 1981.
Work Or the Want of It, 1981.
NGOs Facing Tomorrow, 1981.
The Crisis Now: Commonwealth Government Funding of Non-Government Organizations 1974/75–1980/81, 1981.
Money Matters. A Brief Overview of Current Funding of Non-Government Organizations, 1981.
A Matter of Priority for the 1981/82 Budget, 1981.
Resourcing the Non Government Sector, 1981.
Non-government Welfare Organizations and Poverty, 1981.
Congress of Members Report, 1981.
Unfit for the Pension, 1982.
Congress of Members, 1982.
Welfare: Who Benefits? 1982.
Living on the Edge, 1982.
ACOSS Meets the Prime Minister, 1982.
Distribution in Recession, 1983.
Statement to the National Economic Summit Conference, 1983.
A Commentary on the National Economic Summit Conference, 1983.
Medicare: the Start of Something Better, 1983.
Consultation following the Summit, 1983.
The Assets Test Report, 1984.
Comments on 1984/5 Budget for Combined Unions Conference, 1984.
Understanding Tax Reform, 1985.
Social Justice: The Struggle Ahead, 1986.
Community Volunteer Program, 1986.
Supporting Children, 1986.
National Community Sector Consultation Conference on Income Support for Children: Report of Proceedings, 1986.
Assistance for Families, 1986.
Federal Budget Priorities: 1987/88, 1987.
The May Statement and After, 1987.
Poverty, Wealth and Public Welfare, 1987.
Policies Affecting Sole Parents, 1987.
Effects of Liberals Promised Tax and Expenditure Cuts, and Labour's Promised Family Package on Disposable Income, 1987.

1987 Federal Elections. Assessment of Party Policies, 1987.
Equity and Efficiency in the Business Tax System, 1987.
ACOSS Submission to the Review of Australia's Immigration Policies, 1988.
Extended Care/Health Care, 1988.
Reform of Superannuation Tax Concessions, 1988.
Federal Budget Priorities 1988/89, 1988.
Income Support and Unemployment, 1988.
Child Care: A Background Paper, 1988.
Keeping the Promise: A Strategy for Reducing Child Poverty, 1988.
Return to Full Employment: A Discussion of Employment and Training Strategies, 1988.
Legal Aid at the Crossroads, 1988.
Income Support for People with Disabilities, 1988.
Aspects of Retirement Income Policy in Australia, 1988.
National Liaison Committee on The Child Support Scheme, 1988.
ACOSS Living Standards Package for 1989, 1989.
Federal Budget Priorities 1989/90, 1989.
Improving Retirement Living Standards, 1989.
Privatization and the Human Services, 1989.
The JET and NewStart Programs, 1989.
The Obstacle Course: Workforce Barriers for Pensioners and Beneficiaries, 1989.
The ACOSS Budget Briefing Kit (1989/90), 1989.
Nobody's Children But Somebody's Problem, 1989.
Presidential Address to the 1989 ACOSS Congress, 1989.
Supporting Sole Parents, 1989.
A Home and Community Program, 1989.
Managing Community Services, 1990.
Federal Budget Priorities 1990/91, 1990.
The ACOSS Budget Briefing Kit (1990/91), 1990.
Infrastructure and the Community, 1990.
The Unemployment Crisis, 1990.
ACOSS Election Briefing Kit 1990, 1990.
Micro-Economic Reform and Social Justice, 1991.
NewStart, 1991.
Human Services and Commonwealth/State Relations, 1991.
Federal Budget Priorities 1991–92, 1991.
The ACOSS Budget Briefing Kit (1991–92), 1991.
Directions for National Housing Policy, 1991.
Social Justice and the MFP: The ACOSS Response to the MFP-Adelaide Proposal, 1991.
Rebuilding Health Care or Undermining the Foundations? 1991.
Advance Australia Fair? Recession, Recovery and Social Justice, 1991.
Coalition Taxation and Expenditure Statement, 1991.
Fightback and Low Income and Disadvantaged People. ACOSS Briefing for the Community Welfare Sector, 1992.
Priorities for the 1992 Economic Statement, 1992.

ACOSS Statement on Employment, Education and Training, 1992.
ACOSS Statement on Social Security, 1992.
Unemployment Payment Rates for Young People Must Be Increased: Social Security Budget Priorities 1992, 1992.
ACOSS Budget Priorities 1992, 1992.
Getting Your Teeth into Health Care, 1992.
Healthy, Wealthy and Wise, 1992.
Towards Fairer Urban Growth, 1992.
Submission from ACOSS to National Meeting on Youth Training and Employment, 1992.
Improving Service Delivery to Migrants, 1992.
The Future of Work, 1993.
ACOSS Election Briefing Kit, 1993.
Federal Budget Priorities 1993–94, 1993.
Action on Jobs, 1993.
Beyond Swings and Roundabouts, 1993.
Workforce Barriers: A Discussion Paper, 1993.
Federal Budget Briefing Kit 1993–94, 1993.
Inquiry into The Child Support Scheme, 1993.
ACOSS Submission to Inquiry into the Home and Community Care Program, 1993.
Submission to the Australian Government's Committee on Employment Opportunities, 1993.
Reforming Private Health Insurance, 1994.
Federal Budget Priorities 1994–95, 1994.
Federal Budget Briefing Kit 1994–95, 1994.
Trainee Wages and the Job Compact for Unemployed People, 1994.
Principles for a Youth Income Security System, 1994.
Opening the COAG Door, 1994.
Flexible Families. New Directions for Australian Communities, 1994.
Beyond Charity. The Community Services Sector in Australia, 1994.
The People's Summit, 1995.
Federal Budget Priorities 1995–96, 1995.
ACOSS Response to Industry Commission Inquiry Into Charitable Organizations Draft Report, 1995.
Federal Budget Briefing Kit 1995–96, 1995.
Update: The Industry Commission Inquiry into Charitable Organizations, 1995.
Super, Saving and Inequality, 1995.
Reclaiming The Agenda: Reforming Australia's Community Services, 1995.
Youth Income Support, 1995.
Reforming Australia's Community Services – A Review Of Proposals, 1995.
A Future that Works for All of Us: Goals and Strategies for Australia, 1995.
Call to the Parties, 1996.
Report Of The Study Program On Structural Adjustment And Social Change, 1996.
Submission by the Australian Council of Social Service on the federal government's proposed reforms to the industrial relations system, 1996.

Federal Budget Priorities Statement 1996–97, 1996.
Federal Budget Briefing Kit 1996–97, 1996.
Documents for The National Tax Summit, 1996.
Evaluation of the distributional impact of the 1996–97 Budget on Australian households, 1997.
Young People Gambling & the Internet, 1997.
A common youth allowance, 1997.
Living Wage, 1997.
Radical experiments: the new employment assistance market and service delivery agency, 1997.
Keeping sight of the goal: the limits of contracts & competition in community services, 1997.
Federal Budget Briefing Kit 1997–98, 1997.
People in Financial Crisis, 1997.
People in Financial Crisis 11, 1997.
Loopholes in the taxation of Property & Shares, 1998.
Federal Budget Priorities Statement 1998–99, 1998.
Budget Briefing Kit 1998–99, 1998.
Multilateral Agreement on Investment, 1998.
Agenda for Tax Reform, 1998.
Government's Tax Package ACOSS Analysis, 1998.
Labor's Tax Package ACOSS Analysis, 1998.
Making the Tax Package Fairer, 1999.
People in financial crisis 111, 1999.
Making Good the Promise: Federal Budget Priorities Statement 1999–2000, 1999.
At least 1 million worse off, 1999.
Employment Services Framework, 1999.
A New Lifelong Savings System, 1999.
Negotiating for Fairness, 1999.
Revised Tax Package ACOSS Analysis, 1999.
ACOSS Analysis of NATSEM Tax Modelling, 1999.
Tax Reform and Community Services The State of Play, 1999.
Work, wages, welfare: where is Australia heading? 1999.
Six good reasons not to cut Capital Gains Tax, 1999.
Poverty Factsheet, 1999.
Australians Living On The Edge 11, 1999.
Unemployment Overview 1998–99, 1999.
Work for the Dole – Briefing Paper, 1999.
Finish the Business of Tax Reform, 1999.
The Business Tax Package, 1999.
Common Cause: relationships and reforms in community services, 1999.
Capital Gains Tax Cuts, 1999.
ACOSS Submission To The Reference Group On Review Of The Welfare System, 1999.
Federal Budget Priorities Statement 2000–2001, 2000.
Work, Wages & Welfare: Selected Papers from the 1999 ACOSS Congress, 2000.

Social security breaches: penalizing the most disadvantaged, 2000.
ACOSS briefing papers on the interim report of the welfare review, 2000.
Threshold Issues for Welfare Reform, 2000.
Federal Budget Briefing Kit 2000–1, 2000.
Examining the future of the welfare state and the need for innovative approaches to service delivery, 2000.
Justice & Reconciliation, 2000.
Improving health and well-being requires more than health services, 2000.
Impact of the Revised Tax Package on Australian Households, 2000.
Supporting Families and Strengthening Communities, 2000.
Overview of Employment and Unemployment 1999–2000, 2000.
Public and private sector roles in social services, 2000.
ACOSS 7 Point Plan for Maximum Employment, 2000.
Unemployment and Welfare Reform, 2000.
Australians Living On The Edge 3, 2000.
Doling out punishment: the rise and rise of social security penalties, 2000.
Is the Job Network working? 2000.
Funding Peak Bodies, 2000.
Does Work for the Dole lead to work for wages? 2000.
Flaws in the Government's administrative review proposals, 2000.
Converting waste into welfare, 2000.
Inquiry into the definition of charities & related organizations, 2001.
Submission to the Australian Industrial Relations Commission, 2001.
Just policy, sound research & joint action: Selected papers from the 2000 ACOSS Congress, 2001.
Federal Budget Priorities Statement 2001–2002, 2001.
Benchmarks for Fair Welfare Reform, 2001.
Budget Briefing Kit 2001–2, 2001.
Below-poverty line social security payments, 2001.
Social welfare and social development in the new millennium, 2001.
Breaching the safety net: the harsh impact of social security penalties, 2001.
Riding the roller-coaster: The role of fiscal policy in avoiding and easing recessions, 2001.
A Just and Sustainable Australia, 2001.
Leaping the Chasm: ACOSS Challenge to the Parties for the 2001 Federal Election, 2001.
Australians Living On The Edge 4, 2001.
ACOSS Response to: Australians Working Together – Listening to the Community, 2001.
Flaws in the New Family Payments System for Separated Parents, 2001.
Generating Jobs, 2001.
Research Compendium: Poverty and Inequality in Australia, 2001.
Enabling greater participation by Australians with disabilities, 2001.
Responding to the challenge: The policies of the major political parties in regard to ACOSS Federal Election 2001 priorities, 2001.

Submission to the Productivity Commission inquiry into the Job Network model, 2001.
Ending the Hardship: Submission to the Independent Review of Breaches and Penalties in the Social Security System, 2001.
Strategic Plan 2002–2005, 2002.
Federal Budget Priorities Statement 2002–2003, 2002.
The Obligation is Mutual, 2002.
Submission to the Australian Industrial Relations Commission, 2002.
New Directions for Employment Assistance in the United Kingdom and Australia, 2002.
Federal Budget Briefing Kit 2002–2003, 2002.
A framework for Commonwealth/State Housing Agreement negotiations, and beyond, 2002.
Options for Reforming the Pharmaceutical Benefits Scheme, 2002.
Leaping the Chasm: Selected Papers from the 2001 ACOSS Congress, 2002.
Fairness and Flexibility: Making superannuation work for low and middle income-earners, 2002.
Recognition and justice for asylum seekers, 2002.
Public & Community Housing: A Rescue Package Needed, 2002.
The Bare Necessities: Poverty and Deprivation in Australia Today, 2003.
A charity by any other name. Submission to the Board of Taxation on the draft Charities Bill, 2003.
Rent Assistance: does it deliver affordability? 2003.
Fairness and flexibility: Reform of workforce age social security payments, 2003.
Barriers to university participation, 2003.
Taxation, fairness and public opinion, 2003.
More Affordable Housing, 2003.
Hidden Unemployment in Australia, 2003.
Communities and their capacity to tackle disadvantage, 2003.
Access to Justice and Legal Aid, 2003.
Australians Living On The Edge 6, 2004.
The ACOSS better family incomes package, 2004.
Selected papers from the 2003 ACOSS Congress, 2004.
Federal Budget Priorities Statement 2004–2005, 2004.
Submission to the Australian Industrial Relations Commission, 2004.
Children's Services on the Edge, 2004.
Proposals for reform to student income support, 2004.
For Fairness and Services, 2004.
Housing Services on the Edge, 2004.
Federal Budget Briefing Kit 2004–5, 2004.
More help with the cost of caring for babies and toddlers, 2004.
Submission to the Productivity Commission Review of National Competition Policy Arrangements, 2004.
Australia's social security system: international comparisons of welfare payments, 2004.
Giving Australia: Research on Philanthropy in Australia, 2004.
New data shows private health insurance inequity, 2004.

Submission to Senate Select Committee on the Administration of Indigenous Affairs, 2004.

ACOSS call to the Political Parties, Federal Election 2004, 2004.

Analysis of NATSEM Research on low income families, 2004.

International Comparisons of Anti-Poverty Plans – Lessons for Australia, 2004.

National Community and Social Services Sector Joint Statement Indigenous Affairs in Australia, 2004.

Ten Myths & Facts about the Disability Support Pension, 2005.

Federal Budget Priorities Statement 2005–2006, 2005.

Analysis of waste in the Federal Budget, 2005.

Submission to the Senate Community Affairs Committee Inquiry into the Employment and Workplace Relations (Welfare to Work) Bill, 2005.

Who is worse off? The regional distribution of people affected by the Welfare to Work policy, 2005.

Principles for reform of the Community Development Employment Program, 2005.

Submission to the AIRC National Wage Case, 2005.

Who Cares? Volumes 1 and 2, 2005.

Facts about single parent families and welfare, 2005.

Response to the Government's Welfare to Work proposals, 2005.

Effects of Federal Budget changes for people with disability and single parents, 2005.

Welfare Reform: Participation or punishment? 2005.

Effects of possible changes to the Disability Support Pension, 2005.

Signposts to Welfare Reform, 2005.

Measuring Long Term Unemployment in Australia, 2005.

Giving Australia: Research on Philanthropy in Australia, 2005.

Submission to Senate Select Committee on Mental Health, 2005.

Implications of the Australia–United States Free Trade Agreement: an ACOSS perspective, 2005.

Fair Start: 10-point plan for early childhood education & care, 2006.

Recommendations for the Federal Budget 2006/7, 2006.

Appendix III

Author Interviews and Correspondence

Peter Allen, ACOSS Board member, 30 March 1993.

Richard Alston, Liberal Party Senator, 7 February 1994.

Tony Ayres, Commonwealth Government policy officer, 26 May 1993.

Peter Baldwin, Labor Party MP and Minister, 11 March 1994.

Peter Baume, Liberal Party Senator and Minister, 30 July 1993.

Grant Belchamber, Australian Council of Trade Unions Research Officer, letter dated 7 February 1995.

Colin Benjamin, Victorian Council of Social Service Director, 16 October 1993.

Neil Blewett, Labor Party MP and Minister, 1 February 1994.

John Braithwaite, Economic Planning Advisory Council member, 6 October 1993.

Joan Brown, ACOSS Secretary-General, letters dated 27 June 1993 & 16 November 1995.

Andrew Burbridge, Labor Party Ministerial staffer, 10 December 1993.

Netta Burns, Labor Party Ministerial staffer, letter dated 10 August 1993.

Fred Chaney, Liberal Party MP and Minister, 20 August 1993.

Joan Clarke, Australian Council of Trade Unions Social Justice Committee, 6 September 1993.

Mike Clohessy, ACOSS Board member and Policy Officer, 16 October 1993.

Marie Coleman, Social Welfare Commission Chairman, 18 April 1994.

David Connolly, Liberal Party MP, 28 October 1993.

Julian Disney, ACOSS President, 23 March 1993.

Nigel D'Souza, ACOSS Board member, 27 January 1995.

Graeme Evans, ACOSS policy adviser, 19 October 2004

Adam Farrar, ACOSS media officer, 22 October 1993.

Martin Ferguson, Australian Council of Trade Unions President, 12 August 1992.

Garth Noweland-Foreman, ACOSS Director, 9 July 1993.

John Freeland, ACOSS policy adviser, 22 October 1993.

Murray Geddes, ACOSS President, 8 October 1993.

Major-General Roy Gordon, ACOSS Chairman, 20 March 1993.

Michelle Grattan, journalist, 7 December 1993.

Don Grimes, Labor Party Senator and Minister, 12 July 1993.

Margaret Guilfoyle, Liberal Party Senator and Minister, 1 June 1992.

Patricia Harper, ACOSS Board member, 28 January 1993.

Shirley Horne, ACOSS policy adviser, 12 May 1993

Betty Hounslow, ACOSS Director, 2 March 1995.

Rob Hudson, Victorian Council of Social Service Director, 25 February 1991.

John Langmore, Labor Party MP, 29 May 1995.

John Lawrence, ACOSS Board member, 29 March 1993.

Kate Legge, journalist, 15 September 1993.

Walter Lippman, ACOSS Board member, 15 March 1993.

Mark Lyons, ACOSS Director, 17 June 1993.

Andrew McCallum, ACOSS President, 27 September 2004.

Alison McClelland, ACOSS policy adviser, 3 February 1993.

Paddy McGuiness, Labor Party Ministerial staffer, 5 June 1995.

Bruce McKenzie, ACOSS President, 2 December 1993.

Joan McLintock, ACOSS Secretary-General, 11 July 1993.

Colin Menzies, ACOSS Secretary-General, 11 July 1993.

Merle Mitchell, ACOSS President, 26 February 1991.

Martin Mowbray, ACOSS Board member, 25 October 1993.

Alan Nicholls, ACOSS Board member, letter dated 30 March 1993.

Peter Nolan, Australian Council of Trade Unions Secretary, 10 December 1993.

Edward Pennington, ACOSS Secretary-General, letter dated 2 August 1994.

Reverend Lloyd Phillips, ACOSS Board member, 16 October 1993.

Andrew Podger, Commonwealth Government policy officer, letter dated 5 March 1993.

Michael Raper, ACOSS President, 11 November 2004.

David Scott, ACOSS President, 26 May 1992.

Chris Sidoti, ACOSS Board member, 12 July 1993.

Ian Sinclair, National Party MP and Minister, letter dated 14 August 1992.

Philippa Smith, ACOSS policy officer, 10 November 1993.

Barbara Spalding, Victorian Council of Social Service Director, letter dated 15 September 1995.

David Stanton, Commonwealth Government policy officer, 22 October 1993.

Mike Steketee, journalist, 16 February 1994.

Leon Stubbings, ACOSS Board member, 7 April 1993.

Peter Travers, ACOSS President, letter dated 23 July 1993.

Derek Volker, Commonwealth Government policy officer, 23 March 1993.

William Wentworth, Liberal Party MP and Minister, letter dated 20 June 1992.

John Wheeldon, Labor Party Senator and Minister, letter dated 15 March 1994.

Graham Williams, journalist, 21 September 1993.

Toni Wren, ACOSS media and policy officer, 22 October 1993.

Max Wryell, Commonwealth Government policy officer, letter dated 5 May 1993.

Notes

Introduction

1 Mark Lyons, "Advocacy for Low Income Australians: The ACOSS experience", in *Nonprofit Organizations as Public Actors: Rising to New Public Policy Challenges* (Alexandria: Independent Sector Spring Research Forum, 1995), pp. 682–3; Roselyn Melville, Angela Pratt and Angela Taylor, *The Future of Community Sector Peak Bodies in Policy Making and Advocacy: A Comparative Study of Australian, British and American Peak Bodies within a Neo-Liberal and Market Framework* (Sydney: Centre for Australian Community Organizations and Management, 1998), p. 5.

2 Australian Bureau of Statistics, *Community Services, Australia, 1999–2000* (Canberra: ABS, 2001), accessed <www.abs.gov.au>.

3 John May, "The Challenge of Poverty; The Case of ACOSS", in Marian Sawer and Gianni Zappala, eds., *Speaking for the People* (Melbourne: Melbourne University Press, 2001), p. 254.

4 See discussion of this perspective in *ibid.*, pp. 250–2.

5 Tony Fagan and Phil Lee, "New Social Movements and Social Policy: A Case Study of the Disability Movement", in Michael Lavalette and Alan Pratt, eds., *Social Policy: A Conceptual and Theoretical Introduction* (London: Sage, 1998), pp. 149–51.

6 May, "The Challenge of Poverty", p. 271.

7 *Ibid.*, pp. 253–5.

8 Philip Mendes, *Australia's Welfare Wars* (Sydney: UNSW Press, 2003), pp. 40–1.

9 Australian Council of Social Service, *Annual Report 2004–2005* (Sydney: ACOSS, 2005), p. 6.

10 Trevor Matthews, "Interest Groups", in Rodney Smith and Lex Watson, eds., *Politics in Australia* (Sydney: Allen and Unwin, 1989), pp. 211–27.

11 Paul Whiteley and Stephen Winyard, *Pressure for the Poor* (London: Methuen, 1987), p. 5.

12 May, "The Challenge of Poverty", p. 253.

13 Keith Abbott, *Pressure Groups and the Australian Federal Parliament* (Canberra: Australian Government Press Service, 1996), pp. xi–xvii; Lyons, "Advocacy for Low Income Australians", pp. 691–3.

14 Whiteley and Winyard, *Pressure for the Poor*, p. 13.
15 May, "The Challenge of Poverty", pp. 256 & 262; John May, "The Role of Peak Bodies in a Civil Society", in Adam Farrar and Jane Inglis, eds., *Keeping It Together* (Leichhardt: Pluto Press, 1996), pp. 250 & 260.
16 Bronwen Dalton and Mark Lyons, *Representing the Disadvantaged in Australian Politics: The Role of Advocacy Organizations* (Canberra: The Australian National University, 2005), p. 12.

1 From Voluntary Welfare Coordination to Social Action

1 On the NCSS, see Margaret Brasnett, *Voluntary Social Action* (London: NCSS, 1969).
2 Letter from Joan Brown to author, 27 June 1993.
3 Lois Bryson, "Australia: The Transformation of the Wage-Earners' Welfare State", in Pete Alcock and Gary Craig, eds., *International Social Policy* (Houndmills: Palgrave, 2001), pp. 68–70.
4 Stephen Garton, *Out of Luck* (Sydney: Allen & Unwin, 1990), pp. 141–2; Ronald Mendelsohn, *The Condition of the People* (Sydney: Allen & Unwin, 1979), pp. 125–6.
5 Brian Dickey, *No Charity There* (Melbourne: Thomas Nelson, 1980), pp. 200–3; Garton, *Out of Luck*, pp. 141–2; David Gladstone, *The Twentieth-Century Welfare State* (London: Macmillan, 1999), pp. 49 & 66; Mendelsohn, *The Condition of the People*, pp. 125–30; G. T. Sambell, "Voluntary Agencies in our Changing Environment", in John Lawrence, ed., *Community Service: Citizens and Social Welfare Organizations* (Melbourne: F.W.Cheshire, 1966), p. 5.
6 Adam Graycar, *Welfare Politics in Australia* (Melbourne: Macmillan, 1979), p. 186.
7 Andrew Parkin and Adam Graycar, "The South Australian Council of Social Service", in Roger Scott, ed., *Interest Groups and Public Policy* (Melbourne: Macmillan, 1980), pp. 18–19.
8 "Council of Social Service in Queensland", *Australian Social Work* 12 (1959):44.
9 *Social Service*, October (1946): 8–9; *Kathleen* Shepherdson, "The Vic. Council of Social Service – A Review", *Now*, February (1960).
10 John Lawrence, *Professional Social Work in Australia* (Canberra, Australian National University, 1965), pp. 100 & 184–5. On the key social work role in the formation of the Western Australian Council, see "The Formation of the Council of Social Services of Western Australia", *Australian Social Work* 12 (1959):14–16.
11 Garton, *Out of Luck*, pp. 142–4.
12 *Social Service*, October (1946).
13 Shepherdson, "The Vic.Council of Social Service"; Margaret Kelley, "Victorian Council of Social Service", *Forum: Journal of the Australian Association of Social Workers Victorian Branch* 6, 1 (1952), pp. 1–5.
14 Frank Rowe, "Letter to Miss Lyons", in John Lawrence, ed., *Norma Parkers's*

Record of Service (Sydney: Australian Association of Social Workers, 1969), p. 119.

15 Norma Parker, "Australian National Committee", in John Lawrence, ed., *Norma Parker's Record of Service* (Sydney: AASW, 1969), pp. 123–6.

16 "Australian Council of Social Service", *Social Service* February (1951), p. 32.

17 Norma Parker and William O'Reilly, "Statement Concerning proposed National Social Welfare Advisory Committee", in John Lawrence, ed., *Norma Parker's Record of Service* (Sydney: AASW, 1969), pp. 129–30.

18 *Minutes of the Second Meeting of Social Welfare* Representatives, Melbourne, 25 August 1955; Roy Gordon, *The Australian Council of Social Service*, Unpublished paper (Melbourne, 1993).

19 Anon, "Obituary Hope Clayton MBE", *Impact* 21, 10 (1991), p. 11.

20 Australian Social Welfare Council, *Annual Report 1956–57* (Sydney: ASWC, 1957).

21 Philip Mendes, "Labourists and the Welfare Lobby: The Relationship between the Federal Labour Party and the Australian Council of Social Service", *Australian Journal of Political Science* 39, 1 (March 2004), pp. 149–50.

22 Interview with Major General Roy Gordon by author, 20 March 1993.

23 Gordon, *The Australian Council of Social Service*, p. 3.

24 Australian Social Welfare Council, *Annual Report 1956–57* (Sydney: ASWC, 1957), p. 3.

25 Australian Social Welfare Council, *Annual Report 1958–59* (Sydney: ASWC, 1959).

26 Australian Council of Social Service, *Annual Report 1963–64* (Sydney: ACOSS, 1964), p. 4.

27 Hope Clayton, "The National Role of the Australian Council of Social Service", in John Lawrence, ed., *Community Service* (Melbourne: F. W. Cheshire, 1966), p. 60.

28 See the comments made by Archdeacon Sambell, Tom Brennan, Jean Norris, and David Scott during the panel discussion on social action, *Proceedings of the First National Conference of Social Welfare* (Melbourne:ACOSS, 1960), pp. 73–84.

29 Australian Council of Social Service, *Annual Report 1968–69* (*Sydney*, ACOSS, 1969). On ACOSS' promotion of multiculturalism in place of assimilationism, see Mark Lopez, *The Origins of Multiculturalism in Australian Politics 1945–1975* (Melbourne: Melbourne University Press, 2000), pp. 107–10 & 130.

30 Australian Council of Social Service, *Annual Report 1969–70* (Sydney: ACOSS, 1970), p. 2. See also letter from former ACOSS Secretary General Joan Brown to author, 27 June 1993.

31 Morven Brown, "A summing up of the Conference", in *Proceedings of the First National Conference of Social Welfare* (Melbourne: ACOSS, 1960), p. 92.

32 Australian Social Welfare Council, Fifth *Council Meeting Minutes*, Sydney, 17 February 1958.

33 Australian Social Welfare Council, Fourth *Council Meeting Minutes*, Sydney, 18 June 1957.

34 Sambell, "Voluntary Agencies", pp. 11–12.
35 John Lawrence, "Organizational Issues for Social Welfare" in John Lawrence, ed., *Community Service: Citizens and Social Welfare Organizations* (Melbourne: F. W. Cheshire, 1966), p. 37.
36 Gordon, *The Australian Council of Social Service*, p. 2.
37 Australian Council of Social Service, *Council Meeting Minutes*, 19 August 1961.
38 Australian Council of Social Service, *Annual Report 1966–67* (Sydney: ACOSS, 1967), p. 17.
39 Australian Council of Social Service, *Annual Reports 1966–1969* (Sydney: ACOSS).
40 Letter from Ian Sinclair to author, 14 August 1992.
41 Letter from William Wentworth to author, 17 June 1992.
42 Australian Council of Social Service, *Annual Reports 1956–1970* (Sydney: ACOSS).
43 Ann-Mari Jordens, *Alien to Citizen* (St Leonards: Allen & Unwin, 1997), pp. 132–3; Lopez, *The Origins of Multiculturalism in Australian Politics 1945–1975*, pp. 107–13.
44 Australian Social Welfare Council, *Annual Report 1956–57* (Sydney: ACOSS, 1957) pp. 8–9.
45 Australian Council of Social Service, *Annual Report 1961–62* (Sydney: ACOSS, 1962), p. 9.
46 Australian Council of Social Service, *Proceedings of First National Conference of Social Welfare* (Sydney: ACOSS, 1960), pp. 73 and 80–1.
47 Dickey, *No Charity There*, pp. 204–11; Garton, *Out of Luck*, pp. 149–50; Mendes, *Australia's Welfare* Wars, pp. 17–19; Jocelyn Pixley, *Citizenship and Employment* (Melbourne: Cambridge University Press, 1993), pp. 61–8.
48 Marie Coleman, "Our Pockets of Need", *Australian Social* Work 21, 1 (1968), p. 20; Marie Coleman, "Should Social Workers Go into Politics?", *Australian Social Work* 21, 2 (1968), pp. 27–8; Australian Association of Social Workers and Victorian Council of Social Service, "The National Health Act", *Australian Social Work* 21, 2 (1968), pp. 29–34; Thomas Kewley, *Social Security in Australia 1900–1972* (Sydney: Sydney University Press, 1973), pp. 502–3.
49 Interview with Marie Coleman by author, 18 April 1994.
50 Letter from Max Wryell to author, 15 December 1993.
51 Richard Scotton and Christine Macdonald, *The Making of Medibank* (Sydney: University of NSW, 1993), p. 24; Australian Council of Social Service, *ACOSS Council Minutes*, Sydney, 14 August 1969.
52 Australian Council of Social Service, *Executive Committee Minutes*, Sydney, 16 May 1969.
53 Interview with Lloyd Phillips by author, 16 October 1993.
54 Peter Hollingworth, *The Powerless Poor* (Melbourne: Stockland Press, 1972), p. 21.
55 Australian Council of Social Service, *Annual Report 1969–70* (Sydney: ACOSS, 1970), p. 2.
56 Jean Aitken-Swan, *Widows in Australia* (Sydney: ACOSS, 1962).

57 Joan Clarke, *Just Us: A history of the Association of Civilian Widows of Australia* (Sydney:Hale & Iremonger, 1988), pp. 91–3 and 103; see also statements by MPs Turner and Armitage in *Commonwealth House of Representatives Hansard*, 17 October 1962, pp. 1620–22 & 18 October 1962, 1697–99, and letters of praise from ten parliamentarians cited in Australian Council of Social Service, *Executive Committee Minutes*, Sydney, 8 December 1962.

58 Australian Council of Social Service, *Annual Report 1962–63* (Sydney: ACOSS, 1963), pp. 5–6 and *Annual Report 1963–64* (Sydney: ACOSS, 1964), pp. 9–10; Australian Council of Social Service, *Executive Committee Minutes*, Sydney, 25 August 1962; *Social Service* 14, 6 (1963), p. 1.

59 Garton, *Out of Luck*, p. 147; Gwen Gray, "Social Policy" in Scott Prasser, John Nethercote & John Warhurst, eds., *The Menzies Era* (Sydney: Hale & Iremonger, 1995), p. 215; Thomas Kewley, *Australia's Welfare State* (Sydney: Macmillan, 1969), pp. 100–1.

2 Towards Social Policy Advocacy, 1970–1975

1 See comments of ACOSS President David Scott in Australian Council of Social Service, *Annual Report 1973–74* (Sydney: ACOSS, 1974), p. 5.

2 Interview by author with Joan McClintock, 11 July 1993.

3 Letter from Joan Brown to author, 27 June 1993.

4 Letter from Joan Brown to author, 16 November 1995.

5 Joan Brown, "Influencing National Policy Making", in Greg Mills, ed., *Action for Social Change: Whose Responsibility? Papers from the Eight National Conference of the Australian Council of Social Service* (Sydney: ACOSS, 1974), p. 93.

6 Australian Council of Social Service, *Annual Report 1974–75* (Sydney: ACOSS, 1975), p. 8.

7 Australian Council of Social Service, *ACOSS Action Campaign* (Sydney: ACOSS, 1975), p. 1.

8 Judith Green had represented the NSW Council of Social Service on ACOSS since 1958.

9 Interview by author with David Scott, 26 May 1992; David Scott, "For or Against Materialism", in R. B. Burnheim, ed., *Social Welfare Consequence of Change: Seventh National Conference Australian Conference of Social Service* (Sydney: ACOSS, 1973), p. 61.

10 Interviews by author with Joan McClintock, 11 July 1993 and Peter Allen, 30 March 1993.

11 Letter from Joan Brown to author, 27 June 1993.

12 *Australian Social Welfare*, 4, 2 (1974), p. 13.

13 Interviews by author with Joan McClintock and John Lawrence, 29 March 1993.

14 Jill Wood, "Report from new member of ACOSS: The Council for the Single Mother and Her Child", *Australian Social Welfare*, 1, 3 (1971), pp. 17–18; Anon, 'Agency News: Council for the Single Mother and Her Child', *Australian Social Welfare*, 2, 2 (1972), pp. 10–11.

15 Australian Council of Social Service, *Annual Report 1971–72* (Sydney: ACOSS, 1972), p. 5.

16 *Australian Social Welfare*, 2, 2 (1972), p. 28.

17 David Donnison, "Guest speaker's concluding address", in R. B. Burnheim, ed., *Social Welfare Consequences of Change: Seventh National Conference Australian Council of Social Service* (Sydney; ACOSS, 1973), p. 139.

18 Adam Jamrozik, "Social Welfare as a political power issue", in *Social Welfare Consequences of Change*, p. 132.

19 John Gould, "Analysis of Consumer Group Submissions", *Australian Social Welfare*, 4, 2 (1974), pp. 21–30.

20 *Australian Social Welfare*, 3, 4 (1973), p. 25; Australian Council of Social Service, *Annual Report 1973–74* (Sydney: ACOSS, 1974), p. 10.

21 Australian Council of Social Service, *Are We Second Class Citizens?* (Sydney: ACOSS, 1974).

22 Australian Council of Social Service, *Participation in Australia* (Sydney: ACOSS, 1974), pp. 77–8; Brown, "Influencing National Policy Making", p. 94.

23 Australian Council of Social Service, *Annual Report 1973–74* (Sydney: ACOSS, 1974), p. 25.

24 Jo Murray, "A Consumer Perspective" in Action for Social Change: *Whose Responsibility?*, pp. 98–104.

25 Anon, "Aboriginal champion walks out", *The Mercury*, 24 May (1974).

26 Joan Brown cited in Bob Cameron, "Forgotten million to join forces", *The Sun-Herald*, 27 January (1974); Edward Pennington, "Councils of Social Service – Issues for the Future", *Australian Social Welfare*, 4, 4 (1974), p. 5.

27 Australian Council of Social Service, *Some Developments in ACOSS policies* (Sydney: ACOSS, 1974), pp. 2–3.

28 Australian Council of Social Service, "Taxation and Social Welfare", *Australian Social Welfare*, June (1973), p. 3.

29 ACOSS Constitution, *Australian Social Welfare*, June (1973), p. 24.

30 Australian Council of Social Service, *Poverty: The ACOSS Evidence* (Sydney: ACOSS, 1973), p. 1.

31 *Ibid.*, p. 4.

32 *Ibid.*, pp. 170–1.

33 Pixley, *Citizenship and Employment*, pp. 104–5.

34 Paddy McGuiness, "The poor and the social workers are always with us", *Australian Financial Review*, 16 September (1975).

35 Philip Mendes, "Public choice theory and the de-funding of community welfare groups", *Social Alternatives* 20, 2 (2001), pp. 50–4.

36 Philippa Smith, "The poor need more than cash", *Australian Financial Review*, 23 September (1975).

37 Letter from Joan Brown to author, 27 June 1993.

38 Australian Council of Social Service, *Executive Committee Minutes*, 13 May 1971.

39 Australian Council of Social Service, *Budget Demands* (Sydney: ACOSS, 1975); Australian Council of Social Service, *Australian Budget Process: Documentation*

of Activities in regard to pre-Budget Demands and Recommendations for the Future, 15 August 1975. See also letter from Edward Pennington urging ACOSS national member bodies and the State Councils of Social Service to promote ACOSS' budget demands, 24 June 1975.

40 Australian Council of Social Service, *Annual Report 1973–74* (Sydney: ACOSS, 1974), pp. 13–14.

41 Letter from Joan Brown to author, 27 June 1993.

42 This figure was calculated by the author via a perusal of press cuttings found in the ACOSS archives. See also Australian Council of Social Service, *Annual Report 1971/72* (Sydney: ACOSS, 1972), p. 24.

43 Australian Council of Social Service, *Annual Report 1970–71* (Sydney: ACOSS, 1971), p. 8; *Annual Report 1971–72*, p. 6.

44 L. B. Hamilton, "Address to ACOSS Annual Meeting, 6 October 1972.

45 David Scott, *Don't Mourn for Me-Organize: The Social & Political Uses of Voluntary Organizations* (Sydney: Allen & Unwin, 1981), p. 124; Interview with Marie Coleman by author, 18 April 1994.

46 Australian Council of Social Service, *Annual Report 1971–72* (Sydney: ACOSS, 1972), p. 9; Hollingworth, *The Powerless Poor*, pp. 171–2.

47 Australian Council of Social Service, *Poverty: The ACOSS Evidence* (Sydney: ACOSS, 1973), p. 46.

48 Social Welfare Commission, *Report on the Australian Assistance Plan* (Canberra: Commonwealth Government, 1976), pp. 47–8.

49 Letter from Andrew Podger (former Principal Research Officer for the Social Welfare Commission) to author, 5 March 1993; Australian Council of Social Service, *Annual Report 1972–73* (Sydney: ACOSS, 1973), pp. 6 & 9; *Annual Report 1973–74*, p. 6; Scotton and McDonald, *The Making of Medibank*, p. 137.

50 Interview by author with Paddy McGuiness (former adviser to the Social Security Minister), 5 June 1995.

51 Interview by author with Colin Benjamin, 16 October 1993.

52 See interview with Joan McLintock.

53 Australian Council of Social Service, *Annual Report 1972–73* (Sydney: ACOSS, 1973), p. 11.

54 Tony Hart, "Report of ACOSS 8th National Conference, May 1974", *Australian Social Welfare*, 4, 4 (1974), pp. 19–20.

55 Anon, "Welfare leader criticizes Govt", *Sydney Morning Herald*, 9 June 1975.

56 Australian Council of Social Service, *Annual Report 1971–72* (Sydney: ACOSS, 1972), p. 30.

57 Australian Council of Social Service, *ACOSS Still Fights for a Fair Grant* (Sydney: ACOSS, 1975); *Don't Mourn for Me*, pp. 147–9.

58 Australian Council of Social Service, "A National Inquiry into Social Welfare", *Australian Social Welfare*, 2, 2 (1972), pp. 3–8.

59 Australian Council of Social Service, *Council Minutes*, 19 May 1972.

60 Hollingworth, *The Powerless Poor*, pp. 20–3; Anon, "Church leader calls for poverty study", *Sydney Morning* Herald, 17 July (1972); Max Beattie, "18 bishops rap PM on poverty", *The Age*, 17 February (1972); Bill Hayden,

"Inquiry into Poverty", *Commonwealth House of Representatives Hansard*, 29 August (1972), pp. 826–9;

61 Australian Council of Social Service, *Press Release*, 17 July 1972.

62 Anon, "Social welfare probe needed", *The Age*, 16 June (1972).

63 Anon, "First things first", *Sydney Morning Herald*, 22 August (1972).

64 Anon, "Poverty terms too narrow", *Sydney Morning Herald*, 31 August 1972.

65 Australian Council of Social Service, Press release: "*Proposed National Inquiry into Poverty*", 25 August 1972.

66 David Stanton, "Comprehensive inquiry into poverty", *Social Security Quarterly*, Winter (1973), pp. 27–8.

67 Edna Chamberlain, "Trends in Social Services", *Australian Social Welfare*, 5, 2 (1975), p. 4.

3   Watchdog for the Poor, 1976–1985

1 Australian Council of Social Service, *Annual Report 1975–1976* (Sydney: ACOSS, 1976), pp. 2–3.

2 *Australian Social Welfare – Impact*, 13, 4 (1983), p. 14.

3 Joan McClintock, "Health and poverty", *Australian Social Welfare* 11, 5–6 (1981), p. 32.

4 Interview by author with Colin Menzies, 11 July 1993.

5 Interview by author with Patricia Harper, 28 January 1993.

6 Ian Yates, *Review of ACOSS Roles, Functions, Methods of Operation, and Finance* (Sydney: ACOSS, 1978), p. 1.

7 Letter to author from Barbara Spalding, 15 September 1995; Phillippa Smith and Clare Petre, "Obituary Joan McClintock", *Impact*, October 1996, p. 8.

8 Eva Cox, "The price of reducing poverty", *Australian Society*, 3 December (1982), pp. 21–2.

9 Interview by author with Peter Allen, 30 March 1993.

10 Letter to author from Peter Travers, 23 July 1993.

11 Interview by author with Chris Sidoti, 12 July 1993.

12 Interview with Joan McClintock.

13 Interview by the author with Julian Disney, 23 March 1993.

14 *Ibid.*; Interview by author with Mark Lyons, 17 June 1993.

15 Interview with Patricia Harper.

16 John Lawrence, *Suggested Changes in ACOSS Objects as set out in its Constitution* (Sydney: ACOSS, 1976).

17 Australian Council of Social Service, *Annual Report 1979–1980* (Sydney: ACOSS, 1980), p. 23.

18 Australian Council of Social Service, *Congress of Members* (Sydney: ACOSS, 1981), p. 6.

19 Australian Council of Social Service, *Annual Report 1983/84* (Sydney: ACOSS, 1984), p. 23.

20 Interview by author with Michael Clohessy, 16 November 1993.

21 Action and Resource Centre for Low Income Families, *ACOSS* (Melbourne: ARC, 1979).

22 Australian Council of Social Service, *Annual Report 1980–1981* (Sydney: ACOSS, 1981), pp. 12–13.

23 *Annual Report 1979–1980* (Sydney: ACOSS, 1980), pp. 26–7.

24 *National Taxation Summit Record of Proceedings* (Canberra: Australian Government Publishing Service, 1985); Frank Stilwell, *The Accord and Beyond* (Sydney: Pluto Press, 1986), p. 16.

25 Australian Council of Social Service, *Annual Report 1984/85* (Sydney: ACOSS, 1985), p. 11.

26 Australian Council of Social Service, *Business and the Social Fabric* (Sydney: ACOSS, 1980), p. i.

27 Interview by author with Colin Menzies.

28 Hayden Raysmith, "Goodbye Oliver Twist", *Australian Society*, 1 May 1983, pp. 20–2.

29 Australian Council of Social Service, *Annual Report 1979–1980* (Sydney: ACOSS, 1980), p. 26.

30 Chris Sidoti, "ACOSS: Campaigning for a fair share", *Australian Social Welfare Impact* 15, 1 (1985), p. 13.

31 Australian Council of Social Service, *Annual Report 1979–1980* (Sydney: ACOSS, 1980), pp. 26–7.

32 Australian Council of Social Service, *Annual Report 1984–1985* (Sydney: ACOSS, 1985), p. 4.

33 *Australian Social Welfare Impact* 13, 2 (1983), p. 13.

34 Greg Sheridan, "Lobby groups get the loot", *The Bulletin*, 31 July (1979), pp. 38–9.

35 *Newsweekly*, 12 April (1978), p. 9.

36 Bob Browning, "Business Fails to See", *The Bulletin*, 24 November (1981).

37 Ross Parish and Lisa Gropp, "Welfare Illusions", *IPA Review*, Summer (1984), pp. 185–9; Anon, "The welfare lobby", *Australian Financial Review*, 28 August (1984).

38 David Scott, "Unpublished letter to *The Bulletin*", 26 July (1979). See also Scott, *Don't Mourn for Me – Organize*, pp. 124–5.

39 Martin Mowbray, "Non-government Welfare: State Roles of the Council of Social Service", *Australian and New Zealand Journal of Sociology* 16, 3 (1980), p. 54.

40 See the broadsheet distributed by the socialist welfare workers group Inside Welfare outside the 1978 ACOSS Congress, *Chance or Choice: Who's Kidding Who?*

41 See comments of ACTU Ethnic Liaison Officer and ACOSS Board member Alan Matheson criticizing ACOSS's relationship with big business, "ACOSS Congress", *Australian Social Welfare – Impact* 11, 5 & 6 (1981), p. 22.

42 Mowbray, "Non-government welfare"; Ian Lennie and Pat Skenridge, "Social Work: The Wolf in Sheep's Clothing", *Arena*, 51 (1978); Harry Van Moorst, *The Myth of the Welfare State* (Melbourne: Footscray Institute of Technology, 1984).

43 Philippa Smith, "Advocacy", *Australian Social Welfare Impact* 12, 1 (1982), p. 25.

44 Australian Council of Social Service, *Who Wins, Who Loses* (Sydney: ACOSS, 1979), p. 9.

45 Australian Council of Social Service, *Facts on Welfare* (Sydney: ACOSS, 1980); Philippa Smith, "Riding the welfare tiger", *The Bulletin* 18 September (1979), pp. 68–9.

46 Newton Daddow, "Sharing the load – Churches and the Fair Share Campaign", *Australian Social Welfare Impact*, 15, 4 (1985), pp. 2–4.

47 Australian Council of Social Service, *Annual Report 1982–83* (Sydney: ACOSS, 1983), pp. 16–17.

48 Interview by author with Philippa Smith, 10 November 1993.

49 Alan Nichols, "ACOSS meets the Prime Minister", unpublished report for ACOSS, 24 February 1982.

50 Letter to author from Andrew Podger, Assistant Secretary of the Department of Social Security's Policy Review Branch from 1978–82, 5 March 1993, and interview by author with Senator Margaret Guilfoyle, 1 June 1992.

51 Interview by author with David Stanton, 22 October 1993.

52 Richard Hall, "Hoary old shibboleths tumble", *The Bulletin*, 26 March (1977).

53 Australian Council of Social Service, *Annual Report 1984/85* (Sydney: ACOSS, 1985), p. 14.

54 Peter Beilharz, "The View from the Summit", *Arena*, 64 (1983), pp. 16–21; Randall Stewart, "The Politics of the Accord: Does Corporatism Explain It?", *Politics*, 20, 1 (1985), p. 32.

55 Australian Council of Social Service, *Annual Report 1983–84* (Sydney: ACOSS, 1984), p. 5.

56 Kate Legge, "The man who lost faith in consensus", *The Age*, 18 May (1984).

57 John Short and Jack Taylor, "Crass tax cut battle", *Sydney Morning Herald*, 15 May (1984).

58 Gwynneth Singleton, "The Economic Planning Advisory Council: The Reality of Consensus", *Politics* 20, 1 (1985), p. 20.

59 Colin Menzies, "ACOSS Congress 1984 – Opening Remarks", *Australian Social Welfare Impact* 14, 3 (1984), p. 23.

60 Australian Council of Social Service, "News Release", 28 November (1984).

61 Australian Council of Social Service, *Annual Report 1978–79* (Sydney: ACOSS, 1979), p. 14.

62 Graham Williams, "The Unkindest Cuts", *Sydney Morning Herald*, 22 September (1980); Adele Twomey, "Desperate effort to save service", *Sydney Morning Herald*, 3 November (1980).

63 Australian Council of Social Service, *The Crisis Now* (Sydney: ACOSS, 1981).

64 Australian Council of Social Service, *Annual Report 1980–81* (Sydney: ACOSS, 1981), pp. 23–4 and 27–28; Australian Council of Social Service, *Action for Invalid Pensioners* (Sydney: ACOSS, 1980).

65 Interview by the author with Graham Williams, 21 September 1993.

66 *Australian Social Welfare Impact* 10, 3 (1980), pp. 4–12. See also Philippa Smith, "Advocacy".

67 Interview by author with Fred Chaney, 20 August 1993.

68 *Australian Social Welfare Impact* 11, 2 (1981), pp. 14–15.
69 Australian Council of Social Service, *Annual Report 1981–82* (Sydney: ACOSS, 1982), p. 17.
70 Australian Council of Social Service, *Unfit for the Pension* (Sydney: ACOSS, 1982).
71 *Australian Social Welfare Impact* 12, 4 (1982), p. 13.

4 A Political Insider, ACOSS 1985–1996

1 Tony Moore, "Hawke's big tent", in Susan Ryan and Troy Bramston, eds., *The Hawke Government: A Critical Retrospective* (Melbourne: Pluto Press, 2003), pp. 112–21.
2 Interview by author with Mark Lyons.
3 Peter Browne, "Outside the trilogy", *Australian Society*, May (1986), pp. 16–17.
4 Bill Bartlett, "Sitting on the fence . . . AES and ACOSS", *The AES Report*, March (1991), p. 6. For a similar complaint about ACOSS from a Victorian unemployed consumer group, see Owen Gager, *The Crocodile's Eyes Are Red With Weeping: Unemployed people reply to the Federal Government's Green Paper on Unemployment* (Melbourne: Victorian Social Justice Council, 1994), p. 14.
5 Garth Noweland-Foreman, "ACOSS and the AES – a response", *The AES Report*, March (1991), p. 11.
6 Tim Colebatch, "It's time to plug the holes in the tax bucket", *The Age*, 2 February (1993); Caroline Milburn, "Hope for welfare lobby, says Disney", *The Age*, 13 June (1994); Interview by author with Julian Disney.
7 Liz Fell, "Tax reform; ACOSS takes the running", *Australian Society*, February (1988), pp. 20–1.
8 Liz Fell, "Seven per cent's not good enough", *Australian Society*, November (1988), pp. 26–7; John Langmore and John Quiggin, *Work for All: Full Employment in the Nineties* (Melbourne: Melbourne University Press, 1994), p. 226.
9 Deborah Brennan, *The Politics of Australian Child Care* (Melbourne: Cambridge University Press, 1994), pp. 188 & 192.
10 Australian Council of Social Service, *1989/90 Annual Report* (Sydney: ACOSS, 1990), p. 2.
11 John Freeland, "From redistribution to distribution", *Australian Social Welfare Impact* 16, 6 (1986), p. 11.
12 John Freeland, "Welfare – The Accord and beyond", *Australian Social Welfare Impact* 16, 7 (1986), p. 14.
13 Interview by author with Mark Lyons.
14 Julian Disney, "ACOSS Federal Budget Priorities", *Australian Social Welfare Impact* 18, 2 (1988), p. 2.
15 Lois Bryson, "Welfare's Losing Battles", *Australian Left Review* 107 (1988), p. 32.
16 Sheila Shaver, "Sex and Money in the Fiscal Crisis", in Richard Kennedy, ed., *Australian Welfare: Historical Sociology* (Melbourne: Macmillan, 1989), p. 164.
17 Eva Cox, "The Economics of Mutual Support: A Feminist Approach", in Stuart

Rees, Gordon Rodley and Frank Stilwell, eds., *Beyond The Market* (Leichhardt: Pluto Press, 1993), p. 273. See also Eva Cox, *A Truly Civil Society* (Sydney: ABC Book, 1995), p. 79.

18 See chapter 7 for full details.

19 Padraic McGuiness, "Why welfare is of poor benefit", *The Australian*, 8 October (1991).

20 John Stone, "Restoring trust by speaking your mind", *Australian Financial Review*, 10 October (1991).

21 See, for example, Gerard Henderson, "Behind the endorsement bandwagon", *The* Australian, 27 July (1987); Bob Browning, *The Network* (Melbourne: Canonbury Press, 1990), pp. 178–86, and *Exploiting Health* (Melbourne: Canonbury Press, 1992), pp. 86–91.

22 Mendes, "Public Choice Theory and the De-Funding of Community Welfare Groups".

23 Australian Council of Social Service, *Annual Report 1989/90* (Sydney: ACOSS, 1990), p. 6.

24 May, "The Role of Peak Bodies in a Civil Society", pp. 265–6.

25 Interview with Julian Disney.

26 Milton Cockburn, "Greens failing to see the wood from the tree", *Sydney Morning Herald*, 20 January (1989).

27 Tom Dusevic, "ACOSS sets some ground rules", *The Australian*, 9 January (1995).

28 Mark Lyons, "A View from the Community", in Newton Daddow, ed., *A Fair Share: Report on the National Churches Consultation on Poverty in Australia* (Melbourne: Victorian Council of Christian Education, 1988), p. 89. See also Mark Lyons, "Advocacy for Low Income Australians: The ACOSS Experience", in *Nonprofit Organizations as Public Actors: Rising to New Public Policy Challenges* (Alexandria: Independent Sector Spring Research Forum, 1995), p. 687.

29 See letter signed by Julian Disney for ACOSS and the leaders of four major church groups, "Alarm at growing child poverty", *The Australian*, 3 June (1987). The letter appeared in almost every major newspaper around Australia.

30 Louise Dodson, "The Budget Busters", *Australian Financial Review*, 2 September (1993).

31 Anon, "Cuts unite community and unions", *Australian Social Welfare Impact*, 16, 2 (1986), p. 3.

32 Interview by author with Adam Farrar, 22 October 1993.

33 Interview by author with Mark Lyons.

34 Australian Council of Social Service, *Annual Report 1995/96* (Sydney: ACOSS, 1996), p. 19.

35 Interview by author with Toni Wren, 22 October 1993.

36 Lyons, "A view from the Community", p. 89; Julian Disney, *Presidential Address to the 1989 ACOSS Congress* (Sydney: ACOSS, 1989), pp. 10–11.

37 Interview by author with Rob Hudson, 25 February 1991.

38 Interview by author with Merle Mitchell, 26 February 1991.

39 Industry Commission, *Charitable Organizations in Australia* (Canberra: Industry Commission, 1994), p. 162. On the regular contact of one Social Security Minister with ACOSS, see Neal Blewett, *A Cabinet Diary* (Kent Town: Wakefield Press, 1999), pp. 36–7, 59, 111, 214, 228, 313. For a leading public servant's perspective, see Meredith Edwards, *Social Policy, Public Policy* (Crows Nest: Allen & Unwin, 2001), pp. 31, 64, 131 and 149–50.

40 Interview by author with Garth Noweland-Foreman, 9 July 1993; Interview by author with Betty Hounslow, 2 March 1995.

41 Bettina Cass, "Defending and Reforming The Australian Welfare State", in Lionel Orchard and Robert Dare, eds, *Markets, Morals and Public* Policy (Melbourne; Federation Press, 1989), p. 141; Bettina Cass, "A Family Policy 1983–1995", *Just Policy* 6 (1996), pp. 18–19.

42 Lyons, "A View from the Community", p. 89.

43 Edwards, *Social Policy, Public Policy*, pp. 31 & 131; Fred Gruen and Michelle Grattan, *Managing Government* (Melbourne: Longman Cheshire, 1993), p. 64; Lyons, "Advocacy for Low Income Australians", pp. 686–91. ACOSS's influence on policy outcomes is also acknowledged by former Social Security Ministers Neil Blewett and Peter Baldwin. See interviews by author with Blewett, 1 February 1994, and with Baldwin, 11 March 1994.

44 Julian Disney, "Social impacts of the Hawke years", in Susan Ryan and Troy Bramston, eds., *The Hawke Government* (Melbourne: Pluto Press, 2003), pp. 236–7.

45 Australian Council of Social Service, *Annual Report 1995/96* (Sydney, ACOSS, 1996), p. 23.

46 May, "The Role of Peak Bodies", pp. 269–70.

47 Merle Mitchell, "Politics and policies", *Impact* 22, 9 (1992), p. 2.

48 Industry Commission, *Charitable Organizations*, p. 170.

49 Australian Council of Social Service, *Day of Action on Unemployment Information Sheet* (Sydney: ACOSS, 1992); Adele Horin, "Clever cleric targets MPs on jobless", *Sydney Morning Herald*, 11 May (1992); Mike Steketee, "The flesh and blood jobless to tell their MPs like it is", *Sydney Morning Herald*, 12 May (1992).

50 Anon, "May Day for unemployed", *Impact* 22, 5 (1992), p. 4.

51 Interview by author with Garth Noweland-Foreman.

5 Protecting the Welfare Safety Net

1 Philip Mendes, "Welfare Reform and Mutual Obligation", in Chris Aulich and Roger Wettenhall, eds., *Howard's Second and Third Governments* (Sydney: UNSW Press, 2005), pp. 135–51.

2 Quentin Beresford, *Governments, Markets and Globalisation* (St Leonards: Allen & Unwin, 2000), p. 120.

3 Australian Council of Social Service, *Strategic Plan 1999/2001* (Sydney: ACOSS, 1999).

4 Australian Council of Social Service, *Annual Report 2004/05* (Sydney: ACOSS, 2005), p. 1.

5 Australian Council of Social Service, *Annual Report 1997/98* (Sydney: ACOSS, 1998), p. 16.

6 Rosemary Kusuma, "Local action on unemployment", *Impact*, October (1998), p. 4.

7 Kevin Brennan, "Unemployed people speak out", *Impact* September (2000), p. 5; Kevin Brennan, "Gaining a seat at the table: unemployed groups form national organization", *Impact*, December (2000), p. 1.

8 Australian Council of Social Service, *Strategic Plan 2002/05* (Sydney: ACOSS, 2002), p. 2.

9 For further discussion of the GST debate, see Philip Mendes, "Welfare Lobby Groups and Public Policy Debates: A Case Study of the Australian Council of Social Service and Tax Reform", *Australian Studies* 16, 1 (2001), pp. 143–58. See also Jerome Brown, 'The tax debate, pressure groups and the 1998 federal election", *Policy, Organization & Society* 18 (1999), pp. 75–101.

10 Mark Westfield, "The Business of Balance", in Murray Waldren, ed., *Future Tense* (St Leonards: Allen & Unwin, 1999), pp. 70–2.

11 Australian Council of Social Service, *Making the Tax Package Fairer* (Sydney: ACOSS, 1999).

12 Michael Raper, "Other side of the story is", *The Australian*, 20 July (1998).

13 *Impact* March (1997), pp. 3 and 8–9, and February (2001), p. 5.

14 Andrew McCallum, "Signposts to Welfare Reform", in Peter Dawkins and Michael Stutchbury, eds., *Sustaining Prosperity* (Melbourne: Melbourne University Press, 2005), pp. 110–16.

15 Australian Council of Social Service, *Is the Job Network working?* (Sydney: ACOSS, 2000).

16 *Impact*, November (2001), pp. 1 & 16.

17 Australian Council of Social Service, "A community call for commitment to inclusive and open government", *Impact* October (1998), p. 11.

18 Senate Community Affairs References Committee, *A hand up not a hand out: Renewing the fight against poverty* (Canberra: Commonwealth of Australia, 2004), pp. 6–7, 73, 104–6, 424 & 431–2.

19 Peter Davidson, "Globalization and Poverty in Australia", in Peter Dawkins and Paul Kelly, eds., *Hard Heads, Soft Hearts: A New Reform Agenda for Australia* (Crows Nest: Allen & Unwin, 2003), pp. 47–9.

20 Philip Mendes, "Welfare lobby groups responding to globalisation", *Poverty: Journal of the Child Poverty Action Group* 119 (2004), pp. 13–15 and "A Cross-National Comparison of Welfare Lobby Groups: the British Child Poverty Action Group and the Australian Council of Social Service", *Policy & Society* 22, 2 (2003), pp. 76–97; Interview by author with ACOSS International Policy Advisor Graham Evans, 19 October (2004).

21 Andrew McCallum, "Globalisation and social welfare – the Australian experience", *Address to International Council of Social Welfare Asia-Pacific Region Conference*, December 2003, pp. 13–14.

22 Interview by author with Michael Raper, 11 November (2004).

23 Australian Council of Social Service, *Annual Report 1999/2000* (Sydney: ACOSS, 2000), p. 8.

24 Michael Raper, "Are we creating an underclass?", *The Australian*, 22 January (1998); Darren Gray, "Well-to-do are out of touch", *The Age*, 15 February (2000); Australian Council of Social Service, *Annual Report 1999/2000* (Sydney: ACOSS, 2000), p. 2.

25 Australian Council of Social Service, *Annual Report 2001/02* (Sydney: ACOSS, 2002), p. 2.

26 Anon, "An Invitation", *Just Policy* 6 (1996), p. 2; Anon, "Taxes and social equity", *Green Left Weekly*, 1 May (1996); Marina Cameron, "GST raises its ugly head yet again", *Green Left Weekly*, 21 August (1996); Rosemary West, "To battlers, Harradine is a hero", *The Australian*, 18 May (1999) & "The cost of silence", *The Australian*, 25 May (1999).

27 John Stone, "ACOSS disgraces itself", *Adelaide Review* September (1998).

28 Gary Johns, "Participatory Democracy: Cracks in the Façade", *IPA Backgrounder*, 17, 3 (2005), p. 3.

29 Gary Johns, "Why champions of causes need close scrutiny", *The Australia*, 30 January (2002).

30 Greg Lindsay, "Executive", *Precis* June (2000), p. 3; Peter Saunders and Kayoko Tsumori, "Poor Concepts", Policy 18, 2 (2002), p. 36; Peter Saunders, *Australia's Welfare Habit and how to kick it* (Sydney: Duffy & Snellgrove, 2004), pp. 16–18, 25–7, 124; Peter Saunders, "Lies, Damned Lies and the Senate Poverty Inquiry Report", *Issue Analysis* 46 (2004); Peter Saunders, "Only 18%? Why ACOSS is wrong to be complacent about welfare dependency", *Issue Analysis*, 51 (2004). For further discussion, see Philip Mendes, "The Discompassion Industry: The campaign against welfare bodies", *Overland* 170 (2003), pp. 102–7.

31 Australian Council of Social Service, *Strategic Plan 2002/05*, p. 7.

32 Australian Council of Social Service, "Internal ACOSS Memo" (Sydney: ACOSS, September 2000).

33 *Impact* Spring (2005), p. 3.

34 Mendes, "Welfare lobby groups and public policy debates", pp. 146–8.

35 Richard McGregor, "Cabinet Resistance stalls PM", *The Australian*, 16 October (1998).

36 John Cherry, "Australians Working Together Bill", *Commonwealth Senate Hansard*, pp. 9981–2; Sophie Morris, "Tougher tests for jobless", *The Australian*, 28 March (2003).

37 Rachel Siewert, "Welfare-to-work package flawed", *Press Release*, 26 October (2005). See also *Commonwealth Senate Hansard Community Affairs Legislation Committee*, 21 November (2005), CA24–CA36.

38 Australian Council of Social Service, *Federal Budget Briefing Kit 1996–97* (Sydney: ACOSS, 1996); *Evaluation of the distributional impact of the 1996–7 budget on Australian households* (Sydney: ACOSS, 1997).

39 Benjamin Haslem, "Work plan falls down on the job", *The Australian*, 8 August (2000).

40 Michelle Gunn, 'People's Champion", *The Australian*, 1 November (1997); Anon, "Howard puts faith in big names", *The Age*, 27 November (2000).

41 John Howard, "Address to ACOSS Congress", in *Leaping the Chasm: Selected papers from the 2001 ACOSS Congress* (Sydney: ACOSS, 2002), p. 13.

42 *Impact*, April (1997), p. 3.

43 Australian Council of Social Service, *Annual Report 2000/01* (Sydney: ACOSS, 2001), pp. 1–2, 10.

44 *Impact*, August (2002), p. 1.

45 *Impact*, Summer (2006), p. 3.

46 Australian Council of Social Service, *Annual Report 1998/99* (Sydney: ACOSS, 1999), pp. 3–4 & 11.

47 Fred Argy, *Australia at the Crossroads* (Sydney: Allen & Unwin, 1998), p. 243; Fred Argy, *Where to from Here? Australian egalitarianism under threat* (Crows Nest: Allen & Unwin, 2003), pp. 115–16; May, "The Challenge of Poverty: The Case of ACOSS", p. 256.

48 Australian Council of Social Service, *Annual Report* 2004/05 (Sydney: ACOSS, 2005), p. 8.

49 For further discussion, see Philip Mendes, "Protecting the Safety Net: A Case Study of the Australian Council of Social Service and the Welfare Reform debate 1999–2003", *Journal of Economic and Social Policy* 8, 2 (2004), pp. 25–40.

50 Commonwealth Ombudsman, *Social Security Breach Penalties* (Canberra: Commonwealth Ombudsman, 2002), pp. 1–2.

51 Australian Council of Social Service, *Social security breaches: penalising the most disadvantaged* (Sydney: ACOSS, 2000); Australian Council of Social Service and National Welfare Rights Network, *Doling out punishment: the rise and rise of social security penalties* (Sydney: ACOSS, 2000); Australian Council of Social Service, *Breaching the safety net: the harsh impact of social security penalties* (Sydney: ACOSS, 2001).

52 "Overhaul the social security penalty regime", *Impact*, December (2000), p. 5.

53 Dennis Pearce, *The Report of the Independent Review of Breaches and Penalties in the Social Security System* (Sydney: ACOSS, 2002).

54 *Impact* December (2002), p. 3.

55 Senate Community Affairs Committee, *Report on Inquiry into Participation Requirements and Penalties* (Canberra: Parliament of Australia, 2002), pp. vii–viii, 27 & 47.

56 Kerry Taylor, "Job-seekers get reprieve on penalties", *The Age*, 4 March (2002); Tony Eardley, "The impact of breaching on income support recipients", *Social Policy Research Centre Newsletter* 91 (2005), p. 1.

57 Megan Mitchell, "Runs on the Board", *Impact* Spring (2003), p. 3.

58 John Cherry, "Australians Working Together Bill", pp. 9981–2.

6 Labourists and Welfarists

An earlier version of this chapter appeared as Philip Mendes, "Labourists and the welfare lobby: The relationship between the Federal Labour Party and the Australian Council of Social Service", *Australian Journal of Political Science* 39, 1 (2004), pp. 145–60.

1 Dean Jaensch, *The Politics of Australia* (Macmillan:Melbourne, 1997), pp. 355–9; Marian Sawer and James Jupp, "The Two-Way Street: Government Shaping of Community-Based Advocacy", *Australian Journal of Public Administration* 55, 4 (1996), pp. 82–99.

2 Martin Smith, *Pressure, Power and Policy* (New York: Harvester Wheatsheaf, 1993), pp. 1–7 and 48–75. See also Jeremy Richardson, "Government, Interest Groups and Policy Change", *Political Studies* 48 (2000), pp. 1006–25.

3 Sawer and Jupp, "The Two-Way Street".

4 See further discussion in chapter 1.

5 Australian Council of Social Service, *Annual Report 1962–63* (Sydney: ACOSS, 1963), pp. 5–6.

6 Philip Mendes, "The Victorian AASW's first major social action challenge: the 1965 approach from the Australian Labor Party Social Services Committee", *Victorian Social Work* 9, 2 (2000), pp. 19–20.

7 Connie Benn, "Social Work in the Industrial Society", in Broader Horizons: An Analysis of the Scope of Social Work in Australia, Proceedings of the 10th National Conference of the Australian Association of Social Workers (Sydney: AASW, 1967), pp. 23–39.

8 Scott, *Don't Mourn for Me – Organize*, p. 148; Gough Whitlam, "Inquiry into Poverty", *Hansard House of Representatives*, 29 August (1972), p. 831; Interview by author with David Scott, 26 May 1992.

9 Australian Council of Social Service, *ACOSS Council Minutes*, Sydney, 14 August 1969.

10 Australian Council of Social Service, *Annual Report 1972–73* (Sydney: ACOSS, 1973), p. 5.

11 Australian Council of Social Service, *Poverty The ACOSS Evidence* (Sydney: ACOSS, 1973), p. 46.

12 Lyons, Advocacy for low income Australians, p. 683.

13 Bill Hayden, *Hayden: An Autobiography* (Sydney: Angus & Robertson, 1996), p. 192.

14 Letter from John Wheeldon to author, 15 March 1994.

15 Interview by author with Marie Coleman, 18 April 1994.

16 John Wheeldon, "Estimates Committee", *Hansard Senate*, 11 September (1975), p. 81.

17 *Ibid.*, p. 86.

18 Scott, *Don't Mourn for Me – Organize*, p. 148.

19 Letter from John Wheeldon to author.

20 Australian Council of Social Service, *ACOSS Action Campaign* (Sydney: ACOSS, 1975); Scott, *Don't Mourn for Me – Organize*, pp. 148–9.

21 Peter Baume, "Estimates Committee", *Hansard Senate*, 11 September (1975).

22 John Wheeldon, "Estimates Committee", p. 81.

23 Scott, *Don't Mourn for Me-Organize*, p. 149.

24 Interview by author with Don Grimes, 12 July 1993.

25 *Ibid.*

26 Don Grimes, "The Role of the Welfare Lobby", *Address to 1978 ACOSS General*

Meeting; Dick Klugman, "National Health Amendment Bill", *Hansard House of Representatives*, 7 June 1978, p. 3193.

27 Paul Keating, *Address to National Social Policy Conference*, University of New South Wales, 7 July 1995, pp. 3–4.

28 Brian Howe, "Social Justice – Visions and Strategies', in Duncan Kerr, ed., *Reinventing Socialism* (Leichhardt: Pluto Press, 1992), p. 40.

29 Fred Gruen and Michelle Grattan, *Managing Government*, pp. 63–4.

30 Interview by author with Chris Sidoti, 12 July 1993.

31 Australian Council of Social Service, *Press Release*, 14 May 1984.

32 Australian Council of Social Service, *Annual Report 1984–85* (Sydney: ACOSS, 1985), p. 6.

33 Bruce McKenzie, *Letter to Prime Minister Hawke*, 17 May 1984.

34 Michelle Grattan, "PM in new attack on ACOSS", *The Age*, 24 August 1984.

35 Peter Browne, "Outside the trilogy", *Australian Society*, May (1986), p. 16.

36 Interview by author with Don Grimes.

37 Interviews by author with Don Grimes and Chris Sidoti.

38 See further discussion in chapter 3.

39 Philip Mendes, "NGOs and Public Policy Debates: A Case Study of the Australian Council of Social Service and the last five Federal Election Campaigns", *New Community Quarterly* 3, 3 (2005), pp. 34–5; Peter Walsh, *Confessions of a Failed Finance Minister* (Sydney: Random House Australia, 1995), p. 251; John Warhurst, "Changing Relationships Between Governments and Interest Groups", in Scott Prasser and Graeme Starr, eds., *Policy & Change: The Howard Mandate* (Sydney: Hale & Iremonger, 1997), p. 118.

40 Stephen Mills, *The Hawke Years* (Melbourne:Penguin Books, 1993), p. 27; John Warhurst, "Changing Relationships: Interest Groups and Policy Making in the 1990s", in Andrew Hede and Scott Prasser, eds., *Policy-Making in Volatile Times* (Sydney:Hale & Iremonger, 1993), p. 115.

41 Michelle Grattan, "Keating in clash over delegation", *The Age*, 11 February (1992); Gruen and Grattan, *Managing Government*, p. 64.

42 Michelle Grattan, "GST a tax slug for most", *The Age*, 3 March (1992).

43 Brian Toohey, "Too close to the sun", *Eureka Street*, 6, 3 (1996), p. 15.

44 Simon Crean, "Whose Obligation?", in Just policy, sound research, joint action: Selected papers from the 2000 ACOSS Congress (Sydney:ACOSS, 2001), pp. 27–33; Simon Crean, "Address to the ACOSS Congress 2001", in Leaping the Chasm: Selected Papers from the 2001 ACOSS Congress (Sydney: ACOSS, 2002), pp. 78–82; Wayne Swan, *Postcode* (Melbourne: Pluto Press, 2005), pp. 146–7 and 162–3. See also the comments by Senator Penny Wong cited in Misha Schubert, "Costello's welfare-to-work figures contradicted", *The Age*, 3 August (2005).

45 Brendan Nicholson, "Labor plans to block welfare law", *The Age*, 10 November (2002).

46 George Megalogenis, "Charities' fling endangers GST welfare", *The Australian*, 22 August (1998).

47 George Megalogenis, "Labor threatens welfare lobby on GST opposition", *The Australian*, 20 September (1997).

48 Phillip Hudson, "Unions warn of GST pay battle", *The Age*, 5 February (1999); George Megalogenis, "Keep out of tax blitz: Carmody", *The Australian*, 31 July (1998); George Megalogenis, "Charities' fling endangers GST welfare"; Tony Parkinson, "Tax: does Labor have a credible alternative?", *The Age*, 22 August (1998).

49 Australian Council of Social Service, *Labor's tax package: Fair enough, but not good enough* (Sydney: ACOSS, 1998).

50 Brown, "The Tax Debate, Pressure Groups and the 1998 federal election"; John Warhurst and Andrew Parkin, "The Future of the Labor Party", in John Warhurst and Andrew Parkin, eds., *The Machine* (St Leonards: Allen & Unwin, 2000), p. 12; John Warhurst, Jerome Brown and Rohan Higgins, "Tax Groupings: The Group Politics of Taxation Reform", in Marian Simms and John Warhurst, eds., *Howard's Agenda: The 1998 Australian Election* (St Lucia: University of Queensland Press, 2000), pp. 167–73.

51 Mendes, "Welfare Lobby Groups and Public Policy Debates: A Case Study of the Australian Council of Social Service and Tax Reform", p. 154.

52 Ian Henderson, "If Beazley governed", *The Australian*, 18 August (2001).

53 Luke McIlveen, "Labour's phone price veto bid hurts poor", *The Australian*, 5 October (2002).

54 Mark Latham, "Why it is vital to break the cycle of welfare dependency", *Australian Financial Review*, 9 August (1999); Mark Latham, "Refocus on risk management", *The Australian*, 30 August (1999).

55 Liz Gooch, Jason Koutsoukis and Michelle Grattan, "Welfare body feels Latham wrath on tax", *The Age*, 9 September (2004).

56 Mark Latham, *The Latham Diaries* (Melbourne: Melbourne University Press, 2005), p. 170.

7 Neo-liberalism versus Social Justice

An earlier version of this chapter appeared as Philip Mendes, "Economic Rationalism versus Social Justice: The Relationship between the Federal Liberal Party and the Australian Council of Social Service 1983–2000", *Journal of Australian Political Economy* 46 (2000), pp. 103–25.

1   See further discussion in chapters 1 and 2.

2   Interview by author with Marie Coleman, 18 April 1994.

3   Don Chipp, "Liberal Welfare Policies", *Australian Association of Social Workers News*, May (1976), p. 7.

4   Malcolm Fraser, "Address to Victorian Council of Social Service", 18 September (1975) cited in Australian Council of Social Service, *Future of ACOSS under Threat* (Sydney: ACOSS, 1980).

5   Peter Baume, "Canberra Comment", *Australian Medical Association Gazette*, 18 September (1975).

6   Interview by author with Margaret Guilfoyle, 1 June 1992.

7   Interview by author with Fred Chaney, 20 August 1993.

8   Interview by author with Peter Baume, 30 July 1993.

9   See further discussion in chapter 3.

10 Australian Council of Social Service, *Effects of Liberals Promised Tax and Expenditure Cuts, and Labours Promised Family Package on Disposable Income* (Sydney: ACOSS, 1987); *Coalition Taxation and Expenditure Statement* (Sydney: ACOSS, 1991); and *Fightback and low income and disadvantaged people* (Sydney: ACOSS, 1992).

11 Interview by author with Senator Richard Alston, 7 February 1994.

12 *Ibid.*

13 John Hewson, "de-regulate the labour market, re-examine service delivery", *Policy Issues Forum* November (1991), pp. 2–8.

14 Interview by author with Liberal Party frontbencher (Anonymous), 28 October 1993.

15 Interview by author with Richard Alston.

16 Julian Disney, "The ACOSS response to Dr Hewson", *Policy Issues* Forum, November (1991), pp. 8–10.

17 Richard Appleby, Robert Fitzgerald, Robert Bath and Harry Herbert, "ACOSS work shortchanged", *The Australian*, 11 October (1991).

18 Michelle Grattan, "Hewson's strategy for reform", *The Age*, 13 February 1992. See also James Jupp and Marian Sawer, "Building Coalitions: The Australian Labour Party and the 1993 General Election", *Australian Journal of Political Science* 29 (1994), pp. 20–1.

19 Glenn Milne, "Will to win", *The Australian*, 19 December (1992).

20 John Howard, "Fair Australia", *Address to ACOSS* Congress, Sydney, 13 October 1995.

21 Australian Council of Social Service, *Annual Report 2004–2005* (Sydney: ACOSS, 2005), p. 22.

22 Toohey, "Too close to the sun", p. 15. See also comments of former ACOSS President Michael Raper in Anon, "Howard puts faith in the big names", *The Age*, 27 November (2000).

23 See further discussion in Chapter Five.

24 Tim Pegler, "State refuses to consult: welfare group", *The Age*, 10 September (1996); Michelle Gunn, "People's Champion", *The Australian*, 1 November (1997).

25 Australian Council of Social Service, *Annual Report 1996–97* (Sydney: ACOSS, 1997).

26 "Working with a Coalition government", *Impact*, June (1996), p. 4.

27 Michael Raper, "Social coalition needs social justice", *Impact*, March (2000), p. 3.

28 Petro Georgiou, "Menzies, Liberalism and Social Justice", *1999 Menzies Lecture*, Monash University (1999).

29 Michael Raper, "Libs come clean on welfare", *The Australian*, 23 November (1999).

30 Patricia Karvelas, "Coalition dissent may further soften welfare laws", *The Australian*, 14 October (2005).

31 James Bennett, and Thomas DiLorenzo, *Destroying Democracy: How Government Funds Partisan Politics* (Washington D.C.: Cato Institute, 1985).

32   "Grants to peak bodies announced", *Impact,* July (1997), p. 4; "Peak groups lose funding", *Impact* August (1997), pp. 1 & 4; "A strange understanding of partnership: the Federal Government de-funds peak bodies", *Impact,* August (1998), p. 7.

33   Cathy Moore, "Who calls the shots? – the independence of peak organizations", *Impact* August (1999), p. 12; Marian Sawer, "Governing for the Mainstream: Implications for Community Representation", *Australian Journal of Public Administration* 61, 1 (2002), pp. 44–6.

34   Australian Council of Social Service, *A Charity by any other name. Submission to the Board of Taxation on the Draft Charities Bill* (Sydney: ACOSS, 2003); Sarah Maddison, Richard Denniss and Clive Hamilton, *Silencing Dissent: Non-government organizations and Australian democracy* (Canberra: The Australia Institute, 2004), pp. 2–3.

35   Gary Johns and John Roskam, *The Protocol: Managing Relations with NGOs* (Melbourne: Institute of Public Affairs, 2004).

36   Paddy Manning, "Keeping Democracy in its place", in Margo Kingston, ed., *Not Happy John* (Melbourne: Penguin Books, 2004), pp. 274–6.

37   John Howard, "Tribute to ACOSS on its 40th anniversary", Impact, Supplement December (1996), p. 2; John Howard, *Address to ACOSS Future of Work Conference,* Sydney, 24 May (1996); John Howard, *Keynote Address to the ACOSS National Congress,* Adelaide, 5 November (1998); John Howard, *Address to ACOSS Congress,* Melbourne, 25 October (2001); John Howard, *Address to ACOSS Congress,* Brisbane, 10 November (2005).

38   "Good news for many peaks", *Impact,* February (2001), p. 4.

39   Philip Mendes, "Reconstituting the Public as the Private: John Howard on the Welfare State", *Journal of Economic and Social Policy* 4, 2 (2000), p. 43.

40   Michael Gordon and Tony Wright, "PM lashes the usual suspects", *The Age,* 22 August (1998).

41   Ian Henderson, "Coalition ready to pounce on ACOSS bias", *The Australian,* 28 August (1998).

42   George Megalogenis, "GST fate hinges on $1bn offer", *The Australian,* 28 May (1999).

43   Benjamin Haslem, "Work plan falls down on the job", *The Australian,* 8 August (2000).

44   Amanda Vanstone, "ACOSS inadvertently misleads", *Press Release,* 5 August 2002.

8   A Natural Alliance

An earlier version of this chapter appeared as Philip Mendes, "The Australian Trade Union Movement and the Welfare Sector: A Natural Alliance?", *Journal of Australian Political Economy* 42 (1998), pp. 106–28.

1   David Donnison, *The Politics of Poverty* (Oxford: Martin Robertson, 1982), pp. 133–4; Brian Howe, "Address to 1985 ACOSS Congress", *Impact,* November (1985), pp. 30–1; Brian Howe, "Beyond social democracy: socialism and the

ALP", in David McKnight, ed., *Moving Left: The Future of Socialism in Australia* (Sydney: Pluto Press, 1986), p. 114; Gerry Hand, "Meeting the challenge of the New Right on social policy" in *Proceedings of Australian Council of Social Service 1986 Congress* (Sydney: ACOSS, 1986), p. 38; Council of Social Service of New South Wales, *Australia Reconstructed* (Sydney: NCOSS, 1988), p. 1.

2   Jim Hagan, *The History of the ACTU* (Melbourne: Longman Cheshire, 1981), p. 14; Peter Beilharz, *Transforming Labor* (Melbourne: Cambridge University Press, 1994), p. 40.

3   Francis Castles, *On Sickness Days and Social* Policy (Canberra: Australian National University Graduate Public Policy Programme, 1991), pp. 10–14.

4   Les Louis, *Trade Unions and the Depression* (Canberra: ANU Press, 1968), pp. 156–92.

5   Loucas Nicolaou, *Australian Unions and Immigrant Workers* (Sydney: Allen and Unwin, 1991), p. 24.

6   Hagan, *The History of the ACTU*, pp. 385–6.

7   Gwynneth Singleton, *The Accord and the Australian Labour Movement* (Melbourne: Melbourne University Press, 1990), pp. 61–9.

8   Australian Council of Trade Unions and Australian Labor Party, *Statement of Accord* (Melbourne: 1983), p. 3.

9   *Ibid.*, p. 12.

10 *Ibid.*

11 Randal Stewart, "The Politics of the Accord: Does Corporatism Explain it?", *Politics* 20, 1 (1985), pp. 26–35.

12 Bettina Cass, "Defending and Reforming the Australian Welfare State" in Lionel Orchard and Robert Dare, eds., *Markets, Morals and Public Policy* (Melbourne: Federation Press, 1989), p. 141.

13 Interview by author with Major-General Roy Gordon, 20 March 1993.

14 Australian Social Welfare Council, *Executive Committee Minutes*, 11 January 1956.

15 *Ibid.*, 12 November 1956.

16 Australian Council of Social Service, *Executive Committee Minutes*, 11 March 1960.

17 *Ibid.*, 10 August 1966.

18 Sambell, "Voluntary Agencies in our Changing Environment", p. 11.

19 K. H. McLeod, "Social Welfare and the Trade Union Movement – A Unionist's Viewpoint", in Harold Weir, ed., *Social Welfare in the 1970s* (Sydney: ΛCOSS, 1970); Joan Miller, "Social Welfare and the Trade Union Movement – Current Aims and Policies", in Harold Weir, ed., *Social Welfare in the 1970s* (Sydney: ACOSS, 1970).

20 Australian Council of Social Service, *Annual Report 1969–70* (Sydney: ACOSS, 1970), p. 7.

21 Interview by author with Bruce McKenzie, 2 December 1993; letter to author from Joan Brown, 27 June 1993.

22 Interview by author with David Scott, 26 May 1992.

23 Hagan, *The History of the ACTU*, p. 386.

24 Australian Council of Social Service, *Welfare Under Challenge* (Sydney: ACOSS, 1977), pp. 56–7; Australian Council of Trade Unions, *Executive Report for the Australian Congress of Trade Unions* (Melbourne: ACTU, 1979), pp. 7–8.

25 Mowbray, "Non-government Welfare: State Roles of the Councils of Social Service", p. 57. See also letters of objection to the proposed alliance from ACOSS Board members David Scott and Chris O'Connell, 19 October 1977.

26 Interview by author with Joan McLintock, 11 July 1993.

27 Interview by author with John Freeland, 22 October 1993, and interview by author with Martin Ferguson, 12 August 1992. See also comments of the ACTU Secretary Bill Kelty acknowledging influence of ACOSS on ACTU taxation policy in *National Taxation Summit: Record of Proceedings* (Canberra: Australian Government Publishing Service, 1985), p. 237, and Australian Council of Social Service, *Community Tax Newsletter*, 2 (1985).

28 Peter Browne, "Outside the Trilogy", *Australian Society*, May (1986), pp. 16–19.

29 Australian Council of Social Service, *Annual Report 1986–87* (Sydney: ACOSS, 1987), p. 6.

30 Evatt Foundation, *Unions 2001. A Blueprint for Trade Union Activism* (Sydney: Evatt Foundation, 1995), pp. 274–5.

31 Liz Fell, "Seven per cent's not good enough", *Australian Society*, November (1988), pp. 26–7.; Julian Disney, *Presidential Address to the 1989 ACOSS Congress* (Sydney: ACOSS, 1989), p. 6.

32 Interview by author with Mark Lyons, 17 June 1993.

33 Australian Council of Social Service, *Super, Saving and Inequality* (Sydney: ACOSS, 1995).

34 Australian Council of Trade Unions, *Social Justice Policy* (Melbourne: ACTU, 1995), pp. 43–4.

35 Interview by author with Julian Disney, 23 March 1993.

36 Interview by author with Martin Ferguson, 12 August 1992.

37 Brad Norington, *Jennie George* (Sydney: Allen & Unwin, 1998), p. 241.

38 Australian Council of Social Service and Australian Council of Trade Unions, *Report of the Study Program on Structural Adjustment and Social Change: Stage 1 New Zealand* (Sydney: ACOSS, 1996).

39 Australian Council of Social Service and Australian Council of Trade Unions, *Evaluation of the distributional impact of the 1996–97 budget on Australian households* (Sydney: ACOSS, 1997).

40 Australian Council of Social Service, *Submission on the federal government's proposed reforms to the industrial relations system* (Sydney: ACOSS, 1996).

41 Australian Council of Social Service, *Living Wage* (Sydney: ACOSS, 1997), p. 5.

42 Australian Council of Social Service, *Submission to the Australian Industrial Relations Commission National Wage Case* (Sydney: ACOSS, 2001); *Submission to the Australian Industrial Relations Commission National Wage Case* (Sydney: ACOSS, 2002); *Submission to the Australian Industrial Relations Commission National Wage Case* (Sydney: ACOSS, 2004); *Submission to the AIRC National Wage Case* (Sydney: ACOSS, 2005).

43 Grant Belchamber, "Exploring the real relationship of work, wages and welfare" in *Work, Wages and Welfare: Selected Papers from the 1999 ACOSS* Congress (Sydney: ACOSS, 2000), pp. 5–11; Australian Council of Social Service and Construction, Forestry, Mining & Energy Union, *For Fairness and Services* (Sydney: ACOSS, 2004); Jeff Lawrence, "Towards fair wages and decent work for all Australians", *Impact* May (2003), pp. 12–13; Lisa Heap, "What will result from proposed changes to unfair dismissal laws?", *Impact*, Autumn (2005), p. 10; Helen Creed, "Rights at work", *Impact* Summer (2006), p. 14.

44 Max Ogden, *Towards Best Practice Unionism* (Leichhardt: Pluto Press, 1993), pp. 73–4; Evatt Foundation, *Unions 2001*, p. 237; Sally McManus and Jayne Pilkinton, "The challenge of change", *Australian Options* 1, 2 (1995), pp. 19–20.

45 Gwynneth Singleton, "Industrial Relations: Pragmatic Change", in Scott Prasser and Graeme Starr, eds., *Policy and Change: The Howard Mandate* (Sydney: Hale & Iremonger, 1997), p. 201.

Conclusion

1 Peter Costello, *Intergenerational Report* (Canberra: Australian Government, 2002).

2 Mike Steketee, "The Carrot And The Stick", in Nick Cater, ed., *The Howard Factor* (Melbourne: Melbourne University Press, 2006), pp. 76–83.

3 Philip Mendes, "Empowering the poor: towards a progressive version of welfare reform", *Australian Quarterly* 75, 2 (2003), pp. 23–6.

4 Philip Mendes, "Welfare Lobby Groups responding to Globalization: A case study of the Australian Council of Social Service", *International Social Work*, in press.

Index

Abbott, Tony, 67, 91
Aboriginal and Torres Strait Islander
    Commission, 62
Aboriginal Scholarship Scheme, 12, 25
Aborigines, 23, 47, 59, 62
ACOSS Quarterly, 15, 20
Action and Resource Centre, 34
Alston, Richard, 86, 87
Amalgamated Metal Workers and
    Shipwrights Union, 98
Anderson, Jean, 14
Arndt, Bettina, 65
Association of Apex Clubs, 11
Association of Civilian Widows, 33, 46, 89
Australia-US Free Trade Agreement, 64
Australian Association of Social Workers, 9,
    10, 17, 74
Australian Catholic Social Welfare
    Commission, 89
Australian Chamber of Commerce and
    Industry, 60
Australian Collaboration project, 66
Australian Community Health Association,
    89
Australian Conservation Foundation, 52
Australian Council for Overseas Aid, 16, 36,
    49
Australian Council for Rehabilitation of the
    Disabled, 36
Australian Council of Salaried and
    Professional Associations, 97, 98
Australian Council of Social Service
    funding, 5–6, 13–14, 28–9, 42, 55–6,
    69
    ideology, 23–4, 37, 50, 64–5
    lobbying strategies, 4–5, 26–7, 39–40,
    52–4, 58, 66–7

media coverage, 5, 26, 39–40, 53–4,
    56–7
relationship with government, 12–15,
    27–9, 40–2, 54–5, 67–8
Australian Council of Trade Unions, 35, 49,
    78, 93–102
Australian Council on the Ageing, 36
Australian Democrats, 52, 66
Australian Federation of Consumer
    Organizations, 52–3
Australian Greens, 52, 67
Australian Journal of Social Issues, 15
Australian Labor Party, 4, 17, 30, 41–2, 45,
    54, 72–82
Australian Labor Party/ACTU Accord, 95
Australian Local Government Association,
    53
Australian Manufacturing Workers Union,
    49
Australian Medical Association, 10–11, 17,
    74
Australian Pensioners and Superannuants
    Federation, 1, 23, 33, 46, 89
Australian pre-School Association, 36
Australian Psychological Society, 10–11
Australian Red Cross, 9
Australian Services Canteen Trust, 10–11,
    14, 16
Australian Social Welfare journal, 20
Australian Social Welfare Council, 10, 96
Australian Union of Students, 12
Australian Youth Policy Action Coalition,
    89

Baker, Ron, 59
Bartlett, Bill, 46
Baume, Peter, 76, 84, 85

Brennan, Kevin, 59
Brennan, Tom, 120
Brotherhood of St Laurence, 48, 87, 90
Brown, Joan, 18, 20–1, 25–6, 105
Brown, Morven, 11, 13, 105
Browning, Bob, 38, 51
Bryson, Lois, 50
Burrow, Sharan, 98
Business Council of Australia, 97
business sector, 36, 60

Canadian Council for Social Development,
    7, 12
Carers Association of Australia, 1
Cassar, Judy, 34
Centre for Independent Studies, 65
Chaney, Fred, 43, 85
Charities Bill, 90
Chipp, Don, 74, 76, 84
Clayton, Hope, 11–12, 14, 20
Clerical and Administrative Government
    Employers Organization, 98
Cockburn, Milton, 52
Coleman, Marie, 12, 75
Commission of Inquiry into Poverty, 20,
    22–4, 29–30, 95, 103
Commonwealth Department of Social
    Services, 9–10, 13
Commonwealth Immigration Advisory
    Council, 16
Community Aid Abroad, 12
Conroy, Stephen, 80
Consumers Health Forum, 48
Consumers Telecommunications Network,
    53
Costello, Peter, 67, 90
Cox, Eva, 51

Davidson, Eileen, 14
Davidson, Peter, 80
Day of Action on Unemployment, 56–7
Devine, Frank, 51, 65
Disney, Julian, 33, 46, 52, 53, 79, 99, 105
Donnison, David, 22

economic globalization, 63–4, 104
Economic Planning Advisory Council
    (EPAC), 41, 50
Evans, Gareth, 80

Family Planning Australia, 89
Farrar, Adam, 53
Ferguson, Martin, 99
Fitzgerald, Robert, 46, 79, 80, 88, 105
Forbes, A. J., 14,
Fraser, Malcolm, 76, 84
    Government, 31, 84–5, 95
Freeland, John, 50
Future of Work Commission, 48

Geddes, Murray, 12, 21, 32–3, 105
George, Jennie, 99
Georgiou, Petro, 89
goods and services tax (GST), 60
Gordon, Major-General Roy, 11, 14, 18, 96,
    105
Grassby, Al, 28
Gray, Paul, 51
Green, Judith, 21, 74, 105
Grimes, Don, 76, 78, 79
Guilfoyle, Margaret, 85

Hamilton, L. B., 14, 27
Harper, Patricia, 32–3
Hatfield Dodds, Lin, 105
Hawke, Bob, 41, 54, 78, 79, 94, 97
Hayden, Bill, 25, 28, 74–5, 76
Henderson, Gerard, 51
Henderson, Ronald, 16, 30
Herring, Lady, 9
Hewson, John, 51, 86, 87
Hounslow, Betty, 46, 106
Howard, John, 40, 67, 80, 87–8, 90–1
Howe, Brian, 77
Hudson, Rob, 54
Hunter, John, 11, 15, 105

Inquiry into Charitable Organizations, 49,
    56
International Council on Social Welfare, 9,
    13, 25, 36, 49, 64
Institute of Applied Economic Research, 11
Institute of Public Affairs, 38, 65, 90
invalid pension campaign, 43–44

James, Helen, 11
Jamrozik, Adam, 22
Job Futures Limited, 70
Job Network, 4, 62
Jobs Australia, 70

Johns, Gary, 65
Johnson, Andrew, 106

Keating, Paul, 54, 77, 78, 79

Latham, Mark, 81
Lawrence, John, 15
Lawson, Tony, 33
left-wing critiques of ACOSS, 3, 38, 50–1, 65
Liberal-National Party Coalition Government, 4, 40–1, 58, 67–8, 88–92
Liberal Party of Australia, 83–92
Lippmann, Walter, 12, 16, 26
Loane, Archbishop, 30
Lone Parent Federation, 33
Lyons, Mark, 33, 46, 52, 53, 55, 79, 99, 106

McCallum, Andrew, 65, 105
McClure, Patrick, 91
McGuiness, Paddy, 25, 51, 65
McKenzie, Bruce, 33, 41, 78, 79, 105
McLelland, Alison, 80
McLintock, Joan, 20, 32–3, 76, 98, 105
McMahon, William, 10
Matheson, Alan, 98, 126
Menzies, Colin, 31, 33, 79, 106
Menzies, Sir Robert, 14, 84, 89
Methodist Church, 10–11
Mission Australia, 1, 70, 91
Mitchell, Megan, 106
Mitchell, Merle, 33, 46, 54, 105
Moore, Des, 51
Moylan, Judi, 89

National Council for the Single Mother and her Child, 1, 12, 22–3, 33, 46
National Council of Voluntary Organizations (UK), 1, 7, 12
National Economic Summit, 41
National Organization for the Unemployed, 59
National Shelter, 1, 25, 89
National Tax Summit, 35
National Welfare Rights Unit, 35, 69
National Youth Council of Australia, 15, 36
neo-liberal critique of welfare lobby, 3–4, 25–6, 37–8, 51, 65
New South Wales Council of Social Service, 9, 14, 16, 18

Newsweekly journal, 38
Nichols, Alan, 33
Norris, Jean, 120
Noweland-Foreman, Garth, 46–7, 56–7, 106

Open Family, 87
O'Reilly, Darcy, 10–11, 15, 105
O'Reilly, Winston, 32

Parents without Partners, 33
Parker, Norma, 11
Pennington, Edward, 21–2, 29, 105
People Living with HIV/AIDS, 3
People with Disability Australia, 1
Phillips, Lloyd, 18
public choice theory, 3–4, 25, 85

Queensland Council of Social Service, 8–9, 96

Raper, Michael, 64, 91, 105
Redfern Legal Centre, 43
Rowe, Frank, 10, 13

St Vincent de Paul, 46, 85, 87, 90
Salvation Army, 1, 10, 46, 70, 85, 87, 90
Sambell, Geoffrey, 97, 120
Schools of Social Work, 10–11
Scott, David, 12, 21, 27, 32, 97, 105, 120
Senate Inquiry into Poverty and Financial Hardship, 62
Shaver, Sheila, 50–1
Sheridan, Greg, 37–8
Sidoti, Chris, 33, 37, 77, 79
Sinclair, Ian, 14–15
Smith, Philippa, 25–6, 32, 39–40, 76
Smith Family, 1, 70
Snedden, Bill, 14,
social security breaches, 69–71
Social Welfare Commission, 28, 97
social workers, 1, 8–9, 11
South Australian Council of Social Service, 8
Stanton, David, 40,
State and Territory Councils of Social Service, 1–2, 8–11, 13, 22, 32, 48
Stone, John, 51, 65
Sydney City Mission, 87

Tanner, Lindsay, 81
Tasmanian Unemployed Workers Union, 47
Travers, Peter, 105

Usher, John, 56

Vanstone, Amanda, 91
Victorian Council of Social Service, 9, 14, 16, 32

welfare consumer groups, 1–2, 22–3, 33–4, 46–7, 59
welfare reform, 60–1
Welfare to Work Bill, 61, 68, 104

Wentworth, William, 14–15, 27
Wesley Central Mission, 87
Wheeldon, John, 75–6
Whitlam, Gough, 74
   Government, 20, 27–8, 97, 103
Widows in Australia, 16, 18–19, 73
Willis, Ralph, 97
Womens Electoral Lobby, 53
Wong, Penny, 135
Woods, Frank, 30
Work for the Dole scheme, 61
Wryell, Max, 14, 17

Yates, Ian, 32, 42, 105
YMCA, 10